CHAMPAGNE & CAVIAR & OTHER DELICACIES

CHAMPAGNE & CAVIAR

& OTHER DELICACIES

CELEBRATE WITH THE FINEST LUXURIES

By Judith C. Sutton

Photographs by George Wieser, Jr.

BLACK DOG
& LEVENTHAL
PUBLISHERS

Published by
Black Dog & Leventhal Publishers, Inc.
151 West 19th Street
New York, NY 10011

Distributed by
Workman Publishing Company
708 Broadway
New York, NY 10003

Manufactured in the United States of America

ISBN: 1-57912-038-5

h   g   f   e   d   c   b   a

Library of Congress Cataloging-in-Publication Data

Sutton, Judith C., 1949–
Champagne & Caviar & Other Delicacies/
Judith C. Sutton.
p. cm.
Includes reading list.

ISBN   1-57912-038-5
1. Food. 2. Food—History. 3. Gourmets.   I. Title.
TX357.S88   1998
641—dc21   98-23244
                            CIP

Designed by Jonette Jakobson

Table of Contents

ACKNOWLEDGMENTS

I would like to thank my editor, Pam Horn,
for asking me to embark on
such a wonderful project and for her support;
publisher J.P. Leventhal;
photographer George Wieser, Jr.;
food stylist Kelly Kochendorfer;
designer Jonette Jakobson;
and all the rest of the team at Black Dog.

I would also like to thank the chocolatiers
who were so generous and the other artisans,
purveyors, producers, experts, etc.,
who were so helpful, including, in particular:
Rosario Safina at Urbani Truffles;
Jonathan Morrill, at Tsar Nicolai Caviar;
Richard Donnelley of Donnelley Chocolates;
Christa Vida, at Fran's Chocolates;
Joseph Schmidt, of Joseph Schmidt Confections;
Paula Burdick, of L.A. Burdick Chocolate;
Kathleen Talbert, of Talbert Communications;
and Cathleen Burke, at Kobrand Corporation.
A special thanks to Sandra Jonas, of Caviarteria
for all of her assistance.

Judith C. Sutton

CHAMPAGNE

Dom Pérignon

CHAMPAGNE

"Oh, come quickly, I am drinking stars!"
— Dom Pérignon

It's hard to improve upon the words of Dom Pérignon, the 17th-century Benedictine monk to whom Champagne lovers owe so much, but I'm rather fond of Art Buchwald's description: "I like [Champagne] because it always tastes as though my foot is asleep." In any event, Champagne means celebration, indulgence, luxury. There's always something festive about popping a Champagne cork, something elegant about drinking the bubbly wine from tall fluted glasses. But there is champagne, and then there is Champagne.

When *Larousse Gastronomique* refers to Champagne as a "magnificent wine...[that] has conquered the whole world," it is of course referring to the French sparkling wine produced in the Champagne district, about 90 miles northeast of Paris. The Champenois attribute the unique quality of their sparkling wines to the soil, the climate, the grapes and the particular way the grapes are grown, harvested and turned into wine. In France and in many other European countries, it's illegal to label a wine "Champagne" unless it comes from that district and has been produced using the traditional *méthode champenoise.* Sparkling wines from other areas of France are called *vins mousseux*, while Italy's sparkling wines are *spumanti* and Spain's are *cavas*. In the United States, sparkling wine can legally be called champagne, but many of the better producers avoid the term, instead identifying their wines as having been produced by the méthode champenoise.

Although Dom Pérignon, who was cellarmaster of his abbey for 47 years, is often identified as the inventor of Champagne, sparkling wine had been made in France and elsewhere for centuries before he appeared on the scene. Certain wines naturally referment in the spring (the first fermentation occurs once the grapes are harvested and pressed and turns grape juice into wine), and these had been losing their corks (hence the name *sauté bouchon*, "cork popper") or bursting their bottles for years. Dom Pérignon realized he could save a lot of wine if he used heavier bottles and tied down the corks (he also improved the quality of the corks). Perhaps even more important, he was also responsible for the idea of blending different wines to come up with the delicate, refined Champagne we know today. Although a few French Champagnes are produced only from grapes harvested in a single village, most are blends of up to 30 or even 40 base wines.

All the villages and their vineyards in the Champagne district are graded and classified according to a percentage rating system, ranging from a lower end of about 80 percent up to 100 percent. Only 17 of the almost 300 vineyards have received a rating of 100 percent, which declares them a *grand cru* ("great growth"). *Premier cru* ("first growth") vineyards have ratings of from 90 to 99 percent, and the rest fall into the range between about 80 and 89 percent. (Vineyards that grow both red and white grapes receive a different rating for each.)

Most of the great Champagne houses are located in the towns of Reims and Epernay. Krug, Veuve Clicquot, Mumm, Taittinger, Pommery, Charles Heidsieck, Roederer, and Piper Heidsieck, for example, are all in Reims; Moët & Chandon, Perriër-Jouet, and Pol Roger, among others, are in Epernay. The highly respected Bollinger firm is between these two main centers, just north of Epernay in the small city of Ay, as is Gosset, the oldest Champagne firm of all. (Hautvillers, the historic village that was the site of Dom Pérignon's abbey, is nearby.)

Most Champagnes are a blend of red and white grapes, primarily pinot noir, and, to a lesser extent pinot meunier for the red, and chardonnay for the white. The full-bodied Champagnes called blancs de noirs are made from red grapes only, while the pale, delicate blancs de blancs come from only white grapes. (By the way, those tiny "champagne grapes" at the specialty market really have nothing to do with Champagne—they're just called that because they're so sweet and delicious.) In the Champagne district, a rosé Champagne may be made either by adding a little red wine to the white Champagne blend or by allowing the juices to take on some color from the red grape skins, but elsewhere rosé champagne or sparkling wine is always made with red grapes. (Good rosé Champagnes are full-bodied, slightly fruitier wines that have nothing in common with those awful pink champagnes.) The relatively cool climate in Champagne, which is the northernmost wine district in France, and its chalky, pebbly soil create unique growing conditions resulting in grapes that the French, at least, believe cannot be replicated elsewhere.

When the grapes are ripe, but not overripe (the cool climate tends to prevent grapes from fully ripening), it's time to harvest them and then immediately (to prevent the red skins from coloring the juices) press them. The first pressing yields the top-quality *vin de cuvée or cuvée* which makes the best Champagnes; the *taille*, or second pressing, goes into lesser-quality wines. The juice is then transferred to huge vats for its first fermentation. In Champagne, the winemaker often must add sugar to the acidic liquid to start the process; called chaptalization, this "boost" is standard practice in making French Champagnes, but it's actually illegal in California, where winemakers instead may add specific strains of yeasts as necessary for the same result.

The wine ferments over a period of several weeks, bubbling vigorously at first and finally calming down, ready to sleep through the winter. Once the wine has been allowed to rest, it goes through several rackings—i.e., it is transferred from one container to another, leaving the impurities (lees) behind. Then it is ready for the process that changes it from still wine into Champagne.

First comes the all-important *assemblage*, or blending of different base wines to achieve the desired result. The skill and experience of the *chef de cave* (cellarmaster) of each Champagne house enables him to discriminate among wines he tastes while they are still in their raw state,

Champagne ...
is simply one
of the elegant
extras of life.
—Charles Dickens

Bollinger

determining which ones will result in the type of wine the producer is known for, as, obviously, consistency from one year to the next is essential. The exact blend he finally decides upon, including both wines from that year and still wines from one or more previous years, is known as the *cuvée* (from *cuve*, the French word for vat). Special cuvées may be designated *spéciale* or *grande cuvées*, or *tête de cuvée*.

Most Champagnes are nonvintage, but when the grapes are exceptionally good, the chef de cave may declare a vintage year. Vintage Champagnes, made from a blend of wines from one harvest only, must be aged for at least three years, and are often aged longer. Of recent years, both 1995 and 1996 saw exceptional harvests and were declared vintage years for most Champagne houses; the 1996 particularly will be one to wait for.

Once the specific blending for the cuvée has been determined, the particular wines are blended in large vats (wines that don't make the cut for the cuvée are used for the second-quality Champagnes from that house). Then the *liqueur de tirage*, or *dosage de tirage*, a mixture of sugar and wine, and special yeasts, are added to start the second fermentation. The cuvée is bottled and left to ferment, to build up the carbon dioxide that makes it a sparkling wine. (Wines given a smaller dosage de tirage are less bubbly—these Champagnes are referred to as *crémant*.)

As the wine ferments (even nonvintage Champagnes are left for at least a year), the yeasts eventually die and sediment builds up in the bottles. This must be removed by the process known as riddling or *remuage*. The bottles are placed neck down in special racks that will eventually hold them completely upside down. Over a period of six weeks or so, they are shaken every few days to dislodge the sediment, turned and gradually tilted downward so that the sediment ends up in the neck of the bottle and the rest of the wine is completely clear. (It was Madame Clicquot, "La Veuve [the Widow] Clicquot," who came up with this technique.) Traditionally, riddling was done by hand, by men called *remuers*, the most skilled of whom could turn 35,000 or so bottles a day. Today mechanized racks perform the process in many Champagne cellars; some of these houses, however, still turn the bottles of their vintage Champagnes by hand.

Once all the sediment is in the neck of the bottle, it must be removed by disgorging, or *dégorgement*. This was once done by (very carefully) uncorking the bottle and allowing just the sediment to pour out before (very quickly) recorking the bottle, but almost all producers now use a more reliable method. They freeze the necks of the bottles, then uncork them to allow the frozen plug of sediment to pop out.

Finally the bottles are topped off with the same Champagne to replace what was lost in disgorging and, usually, the *dosage d'expédition* or, often simply the dosage is added before they receive their final corking. Because all the sugar in the wine has been converted into alcohol by the action of the yeasts, the Champagne is very dry at this point. To create different types of Champagne, sugar is added to the wine. Champagnes labeled *nature* or *brut nature* have no added sugar (or only a minuscule amount) and are bone-dry; *brut* (dry) Champagnes have only a very small percentage of added sugar. The classification continues, somewhat confusingly it may seem, through *extra-sec* (extra dry, which might be thought the driest, but is obviously not) and *sec* (dry) to *demi-sec* (semi-dry) and *doux* (sweet). Demi-sec and doux Champagnes are considered sweet or dessert wines.

It's interesting that in this male-dominated industry, women have been responsible for some of the most important developments. As noted above, it was Madame Clicquot who invented remuage, the riddling technique; it was another "Champagne widow," Louise Pommery, who created the first brut Champagnes, having discerned that there was a taste for these drier wines. Before Pommery's Brut Nature appeared on the market in 1879, all Champagnes were much sweeter than the dry sparkling wine we enjoy today.

After the dosage, most of the bottles are recorked, but it is at this point that some

Even for those who dislike Champagne...
there are two Champagnes one can't refuse:
Dom Pérignon and the even superior Cristal ...

— Truman Capote

Champagne may be transferred to the larger bottles known as Jeroboams, Balthazars, and the like (see page 24). Some Champagne may go through secondary fermentation in magnum bottles, but generally the risk of breakage is considered too great to use any larger bottles for the refermentation. The bottles are washed, labeled, then cellared again for a certain period to allow the added sugar to blend with the wine before shipping.

Although the méthode champenoise is by far the best, it's not the only way to make sparkling wine. What is called the transfer method follows the méthode champenoise up to a point, but rather than going through riddling and disgorement, the wine is poured into large tanks and filtered to remove the sediment, then bottled. The tip-off is that the label will read "fermented in the bottle," rather than "in this bottle"; sometimes the labels of sparkling wine produced this way may simply say "bottle fermented" or "transfer method." With the Charmat method, also called the bulk method or process, secondary fermentation takes place in huge pressurized tanks, and only then is the wine bottled. Obviously, this method is far less labor-intensive,and cheaper, than the méthode champenoise, and the grapes used are of lesser quality as well. However, Charmat sparkling wines can be decent. At the bottom of the heap are the sparkling wines made like soda pop, by injecting carbon dioxide into the still wine.

Beyond the Champagne District

The United States, Italy and Spain all have a share of the sparkling wine market. In the United States, most champagne comes from California, but other regions have also begun producing some notable sparkling wines. (The first American sparkling wine actually came from

Veuve Clicquot

Ohio.) Washington State now has more than 80 wineries. Oregon's climate is also favorable to pinot noir and chardonnay, the Champagne grapes. Most of New York State's wines come from the northern Finger Lakes region; Great Western, one of the first champagne producers in America, is here. And recently Long Island wineries have been producing some very good quality sparkling wines.

However, more than 95 percent of all U.S. wines are made in California: Korbel was one of its first producers of sparkling wines, and some of the finest come from Iron Horse, Jordan and Schramsberger. The French Champagne houses have also established a presence in California: Moët's Domaine Chandon has been in operation since the early 1970s, Mumm Napa Valley (its first sparkling wines were labeled Domaine Mumm) produces high-quality champagnes, as does Piper Heidsieck's Piper-Sonoma, and Domaine Carneros is Taittinger's California venture.

Italy's sparkling wine is called *spumante*, which means foamy or frothy. Wines that are not quite as bubbly are described as *frizzante* (lightly sparkling); these tend to be slightly sweeter than most spumanti. Asti spumante is probably what many Americans think of as "Italian champagne," which is unfortunate, for its name

Reims

Paris

CHAMPAGNE
REGION

Château
Thierry

Paris

MARNE RIVER

Vinay

Fontainebleau

SEINE RIVER

CHAMPAGNE
REGIONS OF
FRANCE

N

W   E

S

Reims

Epernay   Châlons-sur-Marne

Vitry-le François

MARNE RIVER

Pont-Ste. Marie   AUBE RIVER

Troys

Krug

conjures up that awful sweet stuff you may have smuggled into your high school prom. But in fact, although Asti (it dropped "Spumante" from its name in 1994, when its classification status was upgraded) is still a sweet sparkling wine, good bottles are now easy to find. Ceretto is one of the top producers.

Both Asti and Moscato d'Asti, which is similar but a frizzante rather than a spumante, are bulk-produced in a variation on the Charmat process. But in recent years Italy has been making a number of excellent sparkling wines following the traditional méthode champenoise (there called *método champenois* or *método tradizionale*). Ca' del Bosco is one of the best producers, Bellavista is another. In Venice, spumante and frizzante *prosecco*, a light sparkling wine that can be dry or slightly sweet, are popular (even in the better restaurants, you may be surprised to find the waiter decanting the house prosecco into a carafe for you). Sparklers from the towns of Conegliano and Valdobbiadene are considered among the best.

Spain's best sparkling wines, or *cavas*, originate in the Penedes district in Catalonia near Barcelona; in fact, the name cava comes from the Catalonian word for cellar. Cavas are produced by the méthode champenoise rather than the cheaper Charmat process. There are indeed some good cavas, but not many, because of the local grapes used for most of these wines. Some of the larger producers, however, use a good proportion of chardonnay and pinot noir, *the* Champagne grapes. Segura Viudas and the high-end cavas from Codorníu and Freixenet are among the better ones.

Serving Champagne

Yes, you can wrest the cork out of a Champagne bottle with a loud pop—or let the occasional overexuberant cork blast out on its own (make sure to point the bottle away from anyone in the room)—but you'll be wasting Champagne, and worse, losing some of the hard-earned bubbles that make Champagne what it is. To open a bottle of sparkling wine properly, first remove the foil covering. Then, with your hand firmly over the cork, twist off and remove the wire cage. With the bottle at a 45° angle and your hand grasping the cork, carefully remove the cork by first turning the bottle—not by twisting the cork—a quarter turn or so until you start to feel the cork begin to loosen. (If you twist the cork, it may break off in the bottle—something you definitely want to avoid.) Then gradually ease the cork out, turning the bottle gently again as necessary, until the cork is

Nebuchadnezzar & Friends

Those oversize Champagne bottles all have specific names; from smallest to largest, they are: a split (a quarter-bottle), a half (obvious), a regular bottle (750 milliliters), a magnum (two regular bottles), a Jeroboam (four bottles), a Methusaleh (eight), a Salmanazar (12), a Balthazar (16) and a Nebuchadnezzar (20 regular bottles).

Disgorging a Champagne bottle the old-fashioned way.

released. (Very occasionally a recalcitrant cork will need extra help, and Champagne pliers are available in upscale wine shops for this task; however, it's rather unlikely you will ever need to resort to them. A device called a Champagne star or key, or Champagne bottle opener, is also available if opening the bottle strikes fear into your heart—but really, it's not that difficult.)

The proper glasses for serving Champagne are either flute- or tulip-shaped ones, which help retain both the bubbles and the wine's bouquet. The shallow bowl-shaped saucers, or coupes, on the other hand, do their best to dissipate the fragile bubbles and bouquet as quickly as possible. (But if for some reason you want only to create a spectacle, you could set up a Champagne "fountain" of several tiers of these glasses, open up a bottle—an early *Joy of Cooking* says a Jeroboam "takes care of thirty-four glasses"—and start pouring it into the top glass so the wine cascades over the sides and into the coupes below. But I wouldn't recommend it.) Make sure your Champagne glasses are squeaky-clean—even a trace of dishwashing soap will kill the bubbles.

If you really want to get serious about Champagne glasses, you may be interested in those from Georg Riedel. While any wine connoisseur knows that red wine, white wine and Champagne should be served in different glasses, Riedel goes much further than that, believing that a glass specifically designed for a certain type of wine will enhance its flavors and bouquet even more. His top-of-the-line "Sommeliers" series of glasses offers 31 different sizes and shapes, including one for vintage Champagne, another for nonvintage and a third for other sparkling wines. (Riedel Crystal of America, Inc. 24 Aero Road, Bohemia, NY 11716; (tel) 516-567-7575; (fax) 516-567-7039.)

Ice Buckets and Other Accessories

Other than the proper glasses, you need little to serve Champagne, since it doesn't even require a corkscrew. However, you may want to consider an ice bucket—not only to keep the opened bot-

Some Champagne houses still turn bottles of their vintage Champagnes by hand.

tle cold, but also to chill it before serving. Most experts agree that overnight chilling, or longer, in the refrigerator actually dulls the flavor of sparkling wine, and recommend no more than two or three hours' refrigeration before serving. But an ice bucket filled with ice and water shortens the process even more, chilling a bottle to the proper temperature—40° to 45° F in about 30 minutes. (Never put a bottle of Champagne in the freezer to quick-chill it; the temperature shock can blunt the taste and dull its character.)

In addition to the Champagne pliers and Champagne star mentioned above, there are a few options if you want to try to keep an opened bottle of sparkling wine alive for up to a day. Champagne stoppers can be used to reseal the opened bottle, and an odd device that looks something like a flattened spoon is meant to be

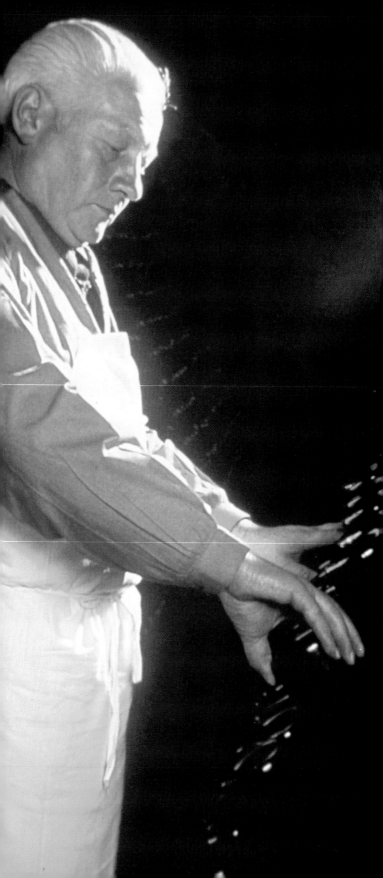

Pommery Louise

*A single glass of Champagne imparts
a feeling of exhilaration.
The nerves are braced; the imagination is stirred,
the wits become more nimble.
A bottle produces the contrary effect.
Excess causes a comatose insensibility.
So it is with war:
And the quality of both is best discovered
by sipping.*

—Winston Churchill

The home of Champagne.

inserted into an opened bottle to preserve the fizz—whether this works or not is debatable, and since it's obviously based on the belief that a teaspoon stuck in the bottle can help keep sparkling wine bubbly, just use a kitchen spoon if you want to try this. But keep in mind that a bottle of Champagne is meant to be opened and enjoyed then and there.

Champagne with Food

Many people save Champagne for dessert, but serving a wonderful brut with chocolate or another sweet is about the worst thing you can do during this course. The sugar in the dessert can make a

dry Champagne taste sour or overpower it completely. The sweeter Champagnes, sec and demisec, work well with most desserts, as do lighter, sweeter sparkling wines like Italy's prosecco and some spumanti. Most experts, however, advise against even trying to match any Champagne with chocolate, which "smothers" the taste buds.

But brut Champagnes go well with many of the other indulgences in this book: Champagne with caviar and Champagne with smoked salmon are classic combinations. Most salty flavors go well with dry Champagnes; oysters are another classic match, and olives, nuts or a cheese like a young Parmigiano-Reggiano will also complement the acidity and bouquet of the wine. You can serve the fuller-bodied brut Champagnes, including the blancs de noirs, with most fish and

Estates in the Champagne region.

Perrier-Jouët

seafood, turkey and other poultry and veal or pork. If you must sip Champagne with your filet mignon or lamb chops, an excellent rosé Champagne would probably stand up best, but it really makes more sense to serve a red wine with these. And if you want to serve a sparkling wine with spicy Thai food or other Asian flavors, stick to extra-dry Champagne or another slightly sweeter sparkler.

Recipes

OYSTERS ON THE HALF-SHELL WITH CHAMPAGNE SAUCE

MAKES 24 HORS D'OEUVRES

2 dozen oysters, well-scrubbed
1 tablespoon unsalted butter
2 shallots, finely minced
1/2 cup Champagne
1/2 cup heavy cream
Salt and freshly ground white pepper

Line a large baking sheet with crumpled aluminum foil. Shuck oysters, reserving their juices and cupped-bottom halves of shells. Place an oyster in each half-shell and arrange on baking sheet, using foil to keep shells level. Strain oyster liquid through a fine sieve.

Preheat broiler. In small saucepan, bring oyster liquid to a simmer over medium-low heat. Add Champagne, bring to a simmer and simmer until reduced by half. Add cream, bring to a simmer and simmer until sauce is slightly reduced and thickened, about 2 minutes. Season to taste with salt and white pepper and remove from heat.

Spoon hot sauce over oysters. Place under broiler and broil until cream is lightly golden brown in spots and oysters are heated through, about 2 minutes. Serve immediately.

CHAMPAGNE SABAYON

Sabayon is the French name for this rich but light custard, zabaglione is the Italian; for an Italian version, use a good-quality prosecco rather than Champagne. This is also good as a sauce served over fresh berries; in that case, the recipe makes enough for six servings.

SERVES 4

4 large egg yolks
1/4 cup sugar
1/4 cup brut Champagne

Combine egg yolks, sugar and Champagne in deep medium size heatproof bowl or in the top of a large double boiler and whisk to blend. Set bowl or pan over barely simmering water (water should not touch bottom of bowl or pan) and, using an electric mixer or whisk, beat until sabayon is very pale, light and thick, (3 to 5 minutes). Spoon into glass bowls or goblets and serve immediately.

VARIATION: Chilled Sabayon with Raspberries: Prepare sabayon as directed, but when removing it from heat, set bowl in a larger bowl of ice water and let cool, whisking occasionally. In small bowl, beat 1/2 cup heavy cream until it just holds firm peaks. Fold whipped cream into cold sabayon and spoon into bowls or goblets. Refrigerate until chilled, 1 1/2 to 2 hours.

CAVIAR

To educate the palate, one really needs to eat a lot of caviar, not with tiny special caviar spoons, but by the solid mouthful.

—Lady Caroline Conran

It's almost inconceivable now, but at the turn of the century, caviar—that ultimate indulgence—was so abundant that saloon keepers would set out bowls of the salty roe on the bar to encourage patrons to drink more. And a 1930s cookbook refers disparagingly to the fact that Woolworth's was stocking caviar at ten cents a tin. Today, because of overfishing and other factors, caviar, like the sturgeon it comes from, is practically an endangered species.

The best caviar comes from the Caspian Sea, which is bounded on the north by Russia and Kazakhstan, on the south by Iran, and from its tributaries. The sturgeon, an oftentimes huge fish with prehistoric ancestors (fossilized remains have been found along the Baltic coast), provides the roe that is processed by time-honored techniques into caviar. Although there are dozens of different varieties of sturgeon, three types provide almost all the caviar we see: the immense beluga, the osetra (also called oscietr or oscietre, from the Russian word for sturgeon) and the sevruga. Caviar from the sterlet sturgeon has always been particularly prized, and today it is the rarest of all.

Caviar (or at least some form of fish eggs eaten as a delicacy) has a long history. *Bottarga*, salted preserved tuna roe, can be traced to the time of the pharaohs, and there is evidence that the art of pickling fish roe was known in ancient Egypt. Aristotle's fourth-century BC writings mentioned the sturgeon, which was featured in Roman banquets, but whether its roe was consumed is unclear. However, Russians have been eating caviar since at least the 13th century. By the Middle Ages, caviar was held in esteem in Italy and other parts of Europe; Shakespeare refers to "caviare" in *Hamlet*, and

French satirist Rabelais mentions "caviat" in *Pantagruel*. But though sturgeon caviar was produced in Italy, France and even Britain, the most prized caviar has always come from the Caspian Sea, from Russian and later, Iranian producers. (Iranian caviar exported in the 1970s was certainly as good as and sometimes better than Russian caviar. However, the Shah's overthrow made Iranian caviar unavailable in the United States.)

The beluga is the largest Caspian sturgeon, growing up to 15 feet long and weighing up to 2000 pounds or more. In a mature female, the precious roe may comprise 10 to 20 percent of its total body weight. The osetra may reach five or six feet and weigh 200 to 500 pounds, while the sevruga is only about 4 $\frac{1}{2}$ feet at maturity, with an average weight of 50 pounds. Sturgeon are long-lived, and part of the reason for caviar's costliness is the length of time it takes females to reach maturity and begin producing eggs. Sevruga mature at eight or nine years, osetra at 12 or 15. Beluga females don't produce eggs until they're 20 to 25 or even older.

Sturgeon may be andromadous (i.e., they live in salt water but swim up freshwater rivers to spawn) or fresh-

water fish. The andromadous Caspian Sea sturgeon spawn twice a year, swimming up the Volga and other rivers to the estuary regions, where they are caught. (In theory, at least; it was not until recently that the countries surrounding the Caspian Sea signed an official agreement prohibiting open-sea fishing.) Each fishing season lasts four months (April through July and September through December); fishermen set up nets in the rivers leading from the sea and periodically check the catch for mature females, easily identified by their swollen bellies. Today, immature females must be returned to the river, but this dictum has not always been followed—another reason for the declining sturgeon population. Once the females are caught, the next steps follow quickly: the sturgeon is taken to a nearby processing center, where the roe will be removed from the live fish (which has either been stunned by a blow to the head or, less commonly, anesthetized). Speed is of the essence, for the membranes holding the eggs will deteriorate rapidly and rupture.

Then the caviar master, whose skills are no less refined than those of the *chef de cave* in a Champagne house, removes the sacs of roe; the fish will be killed, cleaned and prepared elsewhere to be sold fresh, smoked or pickled. First the eggs are strained through a fine screen with openings just slightly larger than the eggs themselves, to remove the membranes and any blood. Then they are gently worked through a finer screen and carefully rinsed. The caviar master is responsible not only for grading the eggs but also for deciding on the precise proportion of salt to be added to preserve them. Size, color, firmness, uniformity, aroma, flavor and texture of the eggs—called "berries" in the trade—all come into play in the master's analysis. Bigger eggs are considered best—beluga is graded from an optimum 000 down to 0—and the lighter-colored caviars, usually from older fish, are considered the finest.

The less salt added, the better: thus the term *malassol*, which does not refer to a specific type of caviar, but rather is the Russian word for "lightly salted." *Malassol* caviar has had only from 3 to

Caviar is to dining what a sable coat is to a girl in an evening dress.
—Ludwig Bemelmans

Caviar and traditional accompaniments, crème fraîche and toast points, with a mother-of-pearl paddle.

5 percent salt (by volume) added to preserve it; the use of term is less strictly regulated in the United States and appears on caviars that are saltier than they should be). Not only will over-salted caviar taste salty, but it also will lose more of its liquid, shrinking and becoming drier, so the caviar master's task is a delicate one. (Some producers use borax rather than salt, which results in less shrinkage and a sweeter taste, but caviar

CAVIAR REGION

Kazakhstan

Volga River

Russia

Caspian Sea

Black
Sea

Turkey

Iran

treated with borax is prohibited in the United States.) Then the caviar is packed airtight in large tins for shipment. The lids are secured with heavy rubber bands to help keep the tins airtight. Caspian Sea caviar is always packed in four-pound (1.8 kilogram) tins; caviar importers and purveyors then repack caviar into smaller tins or jars.

Some producers pasteurize their caviar to extend its shelf life. However, pasteurized caviar doesn't taste as good as or have the consistency of fresh caviar, and caviar lovers avoid it.

Of the three main types of caviar, beluga, as the most expensive, is often assumed to be the best. But judging caviar is in large part a matter of personal taste. There are, however, certain qualities to look for in any type of sturgeon caviar. Start by buying from a shop or dealer that sells a lot of it, so the turnover is good. The tins or jars of caviar should be stored at a temperature between 28° and 32° F (sometimes refrigerator cases have visible thermometers) and the caviar should look pristine. The eggs should be plump whole and unbroken, moist but not swimming in oil. When you open the container, the caviar should have only a faint odor of the sea (if any). And when you taste the caviar, the eggs should offer a slight resistance before popping in your mouth to release their flavor. (But don't be disappointed if some of the eggs don't seem to "pop"—overly firm berries are an indication that the caviar has been pasteurized.)

Because caviar is so perishable, once you've made your selection, most reputable dealers will offer to pack it in an insulated bag or provide an ice pack. Store it in the coldest part of the refrigerator until you are ready to enjoy it. The label may give guidelines for how long you can keep the caviar under refrigeration, but for best results, serve as soon as possible. Once opened, caviar will keep for about a day, no more. (Rod Mitchell of Browne Trading Company recommends protecting opened caviar from the air by gently smoothing the surface of any leftover caviar in its original tin or jar—be careful not to smash the berries—and placing a piece of plastic wrap directly against the surface before replacing the lid.)

A Glossary of Caviar

Here is a guide to the various types of caviar. (For sources, see page 185.)

BELUGA:

Depending on the grade, beluga may range in color from pale gray to almost black. Its berries, or grains, are the largest of the three main types of sturgeon caviar. Grade 000 beluga (sometimes called "prime") is light to dark and the most expensive of the "regular" caviars (some importers occasionally offer rare specialty belugas); grade 00 beluga is darker and slightly smaller. Some caviar merchants sell "broken-grain" beluga at perhaps half the cost of the grade 00. These

Beluga

Imperial

berries, generally from sturgeon caught late in the season, can be flavorful and quite a bargain, but they are soft and do not have the delicious "bite" of the whole grains.

GOLDEN OR IMPERIAL CAVIAR:

Historically the "caviar of the tzars," this is a somewhat confusing category, for not everyone agrees on what this legendary and extremely rare caviar really is. Some say it is from any albino sturgeon—beluga, osetra or sevruga—while others say it is from an older (60 years at least) ose-

Osetra

At the last minute,...
I added caviare aux blinis…
The cream and hot butter mingled and
overflowed, separating each glaucous bead
of caviar from its fellows, capping it
in white and gold.
—Evelyn Waugh,
Brideshead Revisited

tra sturgeon. Majority opinion seems to be that it's the roe of the now almost extinct sterlet sturgeon. When the tzars reigned, by law all golden caviar was reserved for the tzar in power; when Stalin ruled, he received $2/5$ of all the golden caviar produced, with the Shah of Iran receiving another $2/5$ (the remainder went to the chairman of the Russo-Persian Fisheries Company). Rarely seen in this country, golden caviar commands prices that may start substantially above those for beluga.

Of course I seem doomed to live
without actual pain or deprivation, but with undying hope,
from my last taste of caviar to the next one,
so I cannot hold with any tampering with it,
any more than I can approve of sweetened punches,
or "cocktails" made from an honorable Champagne.
There are so many pleasant things to be done with caviar, however,
by people who respect the intrinsic fact that it must
and can stand alone, unaided and unstretched
by such deceivers as minced onion, chopped...
eggs, strips of anchovy.
Perhaps the most impressive such thing I have eaten
is a caviar pie made by a famous amateur chef....
The pie is a gem of simplicity: a baked pastry shell,
filled with about a quart of commercial sour cream...
chives, and then a half pound, or more
of good fresh caviar spread evenly over it.
Come the Revolution...
—M. F. K. Fisher

OSETRA:

Osetra varies more in taste, color and size than beluga or sevruga, but overall it has a fuller, nuttier flavor than either of those two. In fact, many connoisseurs prefer it to beluga. The paler eggs may be sold as golden osetra, not to be confused with golden or imperial caviar.

SEVRUGA:

The smaller gray to gray-black sevruga eggs are the least expensive of the three main types; some people prefer their saltier, somewhat more intense flavor. In general, caviar is best served chilled, if you do want to add sturgeon caviar to a cooked dish, sevruga's grains stand up best to heat.

PRESSED CAVIAR:

Sometimes called *payusnaya*, its Russian name, pressed caviar is made from broken and more mature sturgeon eggs; it is a combination of beluga, osetra and sevruga. It takes four to five pounds of eggs to make one pound of pressed caviar, and the flavor is intense and salty. Some aficionados, however, prefer *payusnaya*'s concentrated flavor—and besides, it's cheaper than sevruga. Its consistency is somewhere between a paste and marmalade.

Sevruga

KALUGA:

Most kaluga caviar is from sturgeon caught in China's Amur River, though some is from Siberia. Although Chinese caviar was once markedly inferior to that from the Caspian Sea and its quality wildly inconsistent, processing methods have been upgraded and now kaluga can be delicious. (Interestingly enough, the Chinese learned how to make better caviar from Mats and Dafne Engstrom, who are now among the pioneers involved in producing caviar from farm-raised white sturgeon in California; see below.) Prices for Kaluga are generally in the same range as for osetra.

Salmon and Other "Caviars"

Until the mid-1960s, American producers could use the term "caviar" freely, even on jars of dyed-black lumpfish roe. However, U.S. laws—and those of many other countries as well—now require that any roe other than sturgeon roe that is called caviar must indicate from which fish it comes. Salmon roe, called red caviar in the trade, is among the best of these other "caviars." The eggs are large (about the size of small peas) and golden-orange in color. The best salmon caviar has a mild flavor and a delightful pop in the mouth. Most salmon caviar in the United States and Canada comes from Alaska and the Pacific Northwest; roe from the chum salmon is the most highly prized.

What is called American sturgeon caviar can vary widely in taste and texture. Although it must be clearly labeled "American," producers are not required to identify the species of fish the roe comes from. White sturgeon, related to the osetra sturgeon, are being farmed in California, and some of the caviar from these fish has been compared favorably with sevruga or even osetra. (One advantage of caviar from farm-raised sturgeon is that quality is relatively consistent.) There are also efforts in other parts of the country to increase production of American sturgeon. Oregon has been producing some very good caviar, though on a small scale, as has Louisiana. The Mississippi River and its estuaries are a major source of American sturgeon caviar; actually, caviar from the Mississippi and elsewhere is likely to be the roe of the paddlefish, another ancient fish but not a true sturgeon. Most American sturgeon caviar has small gray to almost black grains resembling sevruga in appearance, but with a saltier taste. Recently hackleback roe has been appearing in limited quantities; this may range from small dark gray eggs that look like sevruga to larger, paler grains that are closer to osetra in size, and the best can be quite good. With the diminishing supply of, and increasing prices for, Caspian Sea caviar, you may come across other "Caspian-style" caviars in the market.

Some caviar purveyors also market trout eggs, which are about the same color as salmon caviar but half the size. The eggs are firmer than salmon or sturgeon caviar, and the taste is both sweet and salty, with a delicate smoky flavor. The best trout roe is from the Carolinas. Golden whitefish caviar from the Great Lakes has very small, pale orange eggs and a mild, not particularly distinctive flavor. (Incidentally, American golden is the only one of these caviars that can be frozen successfully. Salmon and sturgeon caviars burst and break down if frozen and thawed.)

If there is any "caviar" that truly doesn't deserve the name, it's lumpfish roe, the dyed black or red eggs sold in unrefrigerated jars in the supermarket. It is salty, crunchy, and altogether generally unpleasant.

"That is caviar," she explained to him, "and this is vodka, the drink of the people, but I think you will find that the two are admirably suited to each other."
—C. S. Forester

Champagne or Vodka?

When considering what to drink with caviar, there are really only two choices: Champagne or vodka. Brut Champagne and caviar is a perfect marriage, while good vodka can both underline and smooth the taste of the roe. The Russians, those caviar masters, have of course traditionally drunk vodka with caviar. Whichever you choose, just be sure the Champagne is very dry or the vodka is very cold. Some people like to chill the vodka in the freezer for 24 hours (because of the high alcohol content, it won't freeze, but it will become slightly syrupy) before serving it with caviar, or serve it in a block of ice. Some special caviar servers are designed to hold a tin of caviar and a set of vodka glasses over a bed of cracked ice.

Serving Caviar

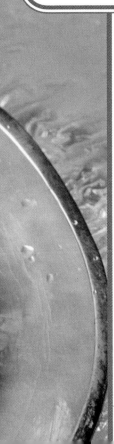

You can present caviar in elegant, specially designed silver servers or dish it right out of the jar or tin—but the one thing you should never do is eat it with a silver spoon: Silver will react with the caviar and give it a metallic taste. Mother-of-pearl or bone spoons, or little "shovels" or paddles, are the choice of most experts, and caviar purveyors and other gourmet shops sell these in a variety of styles, including some with silver-tipped handles. If you want to go all out, there are also gold caviar spreaders available. In earlier days, ivory caviar spoons were rather in vogue (you may be able

Traditional Accompaniments

Although purists and others think caviar needs no adornment and is best served on its own with just a spoon (mother of pearl or bone), there are some traditional garnishes. You can serve any or all of them, or none at all.

Toast points
> (thinly sliced good white bread such as pain de mie, crusts removed, cut into triangles and lightly toasted in the oven)

Chopped hard-boiled eggs—
> yolks and whites chopped separately

Crème fraîche or sour cream

Minced onions

Lemon wedges

Blinis with melted butter are also delicious with caviar (many caviar purveyors sell packaged blinis), but if you don't have toast points or blinis, don't be tempted to serve caviar with crackers—they're too crisp, and you'll miss out on that delicate "pop" as the berries burst in your mouth.

[on Christmas dinner]:
...I am apt to go all out and spend money with no thought of tomorrow. One of my favorite extravagances is to have a hearty supply of fresh caviar with lemon and plenty of crisp toast and, for those who really must have them, chopped onion and sour cream. With this I like vodka, chilled in the freezer until icy cold. Then, after everyone has had their fill of caviar,...

—James Beard

*Caviar accoutrements
(from top to bottom):
silver-trimmed server, to be filled with ice;
individual servers
(the one on the right is designed to hold ice);
small and large mother-of-pearl plates;
mother-of-pearl spoons.*

to find them in antique shops). Lacking any of these, plastic spoons, somewhat disconcertingly, are really the best alternative, because they will not affect the taste of the caviar; some importers, in fact, do all their personal tasting with the type of mini plastic spoons you are offered when you ask for a sample at an ice cream shop.

The traditional way to serve caviar is straight from the tin, nestled in a bowl of crushed or shaved ice. For a tasting, some caviar servers are designed to hold one or more, one-ounce jars, while with others (which may be made of glass, often trimmed with silver, or mother of pearl), you transfer the caviar to the server. Some of these have space for shaved ice, some don't.

How much caviar to serve? One ounce per person is considered reasonable, but for some people, less than two ounces just will not do. For a sampling of the three types of caviar to be indulged in with one other person, an ounce each of sevruga, osetra and beluga would be quite nice. But for some, there is no such thing as too much caviar. M. F. K. Fisher once lamented,"... I have dug into a one-pound tin of (Beluga caviar), fresh and pearly gray, not more than eight or nine times in my life...."

Tiny New Potatoes with Crème Fraîche & Caviar

Makes 24 hors d'oeuvres

24 tiny white new potatoes
  (about 1 inch across; about 1 pound)
About ½ cup crème fraîche
2 to 4 ounces caviar

Put potatoes in a large pot, add water to cover by about 2 inches, add generous pinch of salt and bring to a boil over high heat. Boil gently until potatoes are tender, 18 to 20 minutes. Drain and let cool slightly.

(Potatoes can be cooked up to 2 hours ahead and set aside at room temperature.)

Cut a small slice off the bottom of each potato so it will sit upright, then slice off the top quarter. Mound a scant teaspoonful of crème fraîche on top, then top with caviar. Serve immediately.

When I was young and poor,
my favorite dish was caviar accompanied by
a half bottle of Bollinger.
But repetition destroys any pleasure,
gastronomic or sexual...

—A. J. Cronin

Oysters on the Half-Shell with Caviar

MAKES 24 HORS D'OEUVRES

Kosher salt
24 oysters, well scrubbed
2 to 3 ounces caviar

Spread a ¼-inch-thick layer of kosher salt on bottom of 2 large serving plates. Shuck oysters, discarding top shells and leaving oysters and their juices in cupped bottom halves of shells (but do loosen oysters from bottom shells).

Arrange oysters on serving plates. Spoon a dollop of caviar onto each and serve. (If you'd rather serve one platter at a time, garnish only one platter with caviar. Cover second platter with plastic wrap and refrigerate; garnish with remaining caviar just before serving.)

Mini Potato Pancakes with Crème Fraîche & Caviar

Makes about 24 hors d'oeuvres

1 small-to-medium baking potato (8 ounces)
1 large egg
1 1/2 tablespoons all-purpose flour
3/8 teaspoon salt
1/2 teaspoon freshly ground black pepper
Vegetable oil for frying
About 1 1/4 cups crème fraîche
2 ounces caviar

Wash, peel and grate potato. Place grated potato in a sieve, rinse well under cold water and drain thoroughly. With your hands, squeeze potato as dry as possible. In a medium bowl, combine potato, egg, flour, salt and pepper and stir to mix well.

In a large heavy frying pan, heat 1/4 inch of oil over medium-high heat until oil is very hot but not smoking. Stir potato mixture and drop it by generous teaspoonfuls into the hot oil, without crowding. Flatten pancakes slightly with spoon back and cook until golden brown on the bottom, about 3 minutes. Turn cakes and cook until golden brown on both sides, about 3 minutes longer. Transfer to paper towels to drain, and repeat process with remaining mixture, stirring each time before using it. (Pancakes are best served as soon as they are made, but if necessary can be kept warm on a paper towel-lined baking sheet in a 200° F oven for up to 30 minutes.)

Top each pancake with a scant tablespoon of crème fraîche and a small dollop of caviar. Serve immediately.

...I was perhaps twenty-three
when I first ate almost enough caviar
—not to mention any caviar at all
that I can now remember.
It was one of the best, brightest days
of my whole life with my parents....
My father and I ate caviar, probably sevruga,
with green-black smallish beads
and a superb challenge of flavor
for the iced grassy vodka we used
to cleanse our happy palates.
We ate three portions apiece,
tacitly knowing it could never happen again
that anything would be quite so
mysteriously perfect in both time and space.
The headwaiter sensed all this...
and the portions got larger,
and at our third blissful command
he simply put the tin
in its ice bowl upon our table.
It was a regal gesture, like being tapped
on the shoulder with a sword.

—M. F. K. Fisher

CREAMY BROILED OYSTERS WITH CAVIAR

MAKES 24 HORS D'OEUVRES

24 oysters, well scrubbed
1/2 cup heavy cream
Salt and freshly ground white pepper
2 to 3 ounces caviar

Line a large baking sheet with crumpled aluminum foil. Shuck oysters, reserving their juices and cupped-bottom halves of shells. Place an oyster in each half-shell and arrange on baking sheet, using foil to keep shells level. Strain oyster liquid through a fine sieve into a bowl.

Preheat broiler. In a small saucepan, bring oyster liquid to a simmer over medium-low heat. Add cream, bring to a simmer and simmer, stirring occasionally, until sauce is slightly reduced and thickened, about 2 minutes. Season to taste with salt and white pepper and remove from heat.

Spoon hot cream sauce over oysters. Place under broiler and broil until cream is lightly golden brown in spots and oysters are heated through, about 2 minutes. Spoon a dollop of caviar onto each oyster and serve immediately.

FRENCH SCRAMBLED EGGS WITH CAVIAR

Cooking eggs this way makes them incredibly creamy and smooth. Scrambled eggs and caviar is served as a first course at elegant French restaurants; the combination is wonderfully indulgent for a weekend breakfast or brunch.

SERVES 2

5 large eggs
2 tablespoons heavy cream
Salt and freshly ground black pepper
1 1/2 tablespoons unsalted butter
2 to 3 teaspoons (or more) caviar

In a medium bowl, beat eggs with cream and salt and pepper to taste. Melt butter in a medium frying pan over low heat. Add eggs and cook, whisking constantly, until eggs are very creamy and just set, about 5 minutes. Arrange the eggs on 2 serving plates. Spoon caviar over eggs and serve immediately.

...As for the caviar, I can wait.
I know I cannot possibly, ever, eat enough of it to satisfy my
hunger, my unreasonable lust, so I think back
with what is almost placidity upon the times I could attack
a tub of it and take five minutes or so for every
small voluptuous mouthful. Again, why not?—

M. F. K. Fisher

SMOKED STURGEON WITH SEVRUGA CAVIAR SAUCE

This elegant but very simple sauce would also be good served
with grilled swordfish or pan-seared halibut steaks. Substitute
good-quality American sturgeon caviar for the sevruga if you'd like.

SERVES 4 AS AN APPETIZER

1 ½ teaspoons unsalted butter
2 scallions (white part only), finely chopped
⅓ cup chicken stock
½ cup crème fraîche
1 ounce sevruga caviar
Salt and freshly ground black pepper
¾ pound smoked sturgeon, thinly sliced
Chopped chives for garnish

Melt butter in small frying pan over medium-low heat. Add scallions and cook, stirring occasionally, until scallions are very soft, about 5 minutes. Add chicken stock, increase heat to medium and bring to a simmer. Simmer until stock is reduced almost to a glaze, about 3 minutes. Stir in crème fraîche and simmer, stirring occasionally, until slightly reduced and thickened, 2 to 3 minutes. Remove from heat and let cool slightly.

Meanwhile, arrange smoked sturgeon on 4 serving plates.

Add half the caviar to cream sauce, stirring gently just to mix. Season to taste with salt and pepper. Spoon sauce over smoked sturgeon and spoon remaining caviar over sauce. Sprinkle with chives and serve immediately.

Oyster Pan-Roast with Watercress & Caviar

The peppery, slightly bitter watercress is the perfect counterpoint to the richness of the creamy oyster stew.

SERVES 4 AS AN APPETIZER

2 dozen oysters, shucked and liquid reserved
1 cup heavy cream
Salt and freshly ground white pepper
12 large sprigs watercress
2 ounces sevruga caviar

In a small saucepan, combine reserved oyster liquid and cream and bring to a simmer over medium-low heat. Add oysters and simmer gently until cream mixture is slightly reduced and thickened and oysters begin to curl, about 2 minutes. Season to taste with salt and white pepper and remove from heat.

Arrange oysters in 4 shallow soup plates. Spoon cream mixture into bowls and garnish each with 3 sprigs of watercress. Top each oyster with a small dollop of caviar and serve immediately.

CHOCOLATE

The botanical name for the cacao tree, the source of chocolate, is *Theobroma cacao, theobroma* meaning "food of the gods"—a designation with which many of us would certainly agree. The enjoyment of chocolate as an indulgent luxury can be traced back centuries, for the Aztecs are known to have revered chocolate as "the drink of the gods"; they also called it "liquid gold." When the Spanish explorer Hernando Cortés arrived in Mexico in the early 16th century, he found the thriving Aztec civilization, with its capital in what is now Mexico City. The emperor Montezuma entertained Cortés and his entourage at a series of lavish banquets, where they were served a frothy chocolate drink in golden goblets. The Aztecs, who also used cacao beans as currency, regarded chocolate as both a source of energy and an aphrodisiac (reserved for men), and Cortés found it to be reviving as well.

However, the beverage served at the court of Montezuma was far removed from the hot chocolate we know today. Its name, *xocolatl,* means "bitter water," and it certainly was, although chiles and spices, and sometimes vanilla, were added to flavor it. Cortés took the idea back to Spain with him, but chocolate was not at first greeted with much enthusiasm (in fact, Columbus had brought cacao beans back to the Spanish court several decades before Cortés did, but their bitter flavor had little appeal). Once the Spanish added sugar to the drink, however, it was another matter, and chocolate sweetened with sugar and flavored with vanilla soon became popular with those who could afford it, as it was expensive. Despite its newly sweetened flavor, however, it was still regarded as a tonic or restorative.

Chocolate was little known outside Spain until the early 1600s, but by the middle of that century, it was popular throughout Europe. Yet not everyone (again, of those who could afford the expense) was enamored of its flavor, and although it was served in coffee houses, its reputation as a medicinal drink with healthful benefits remained intact. Gradually, however, it evolved into a sweeter rather than spicy drink, and both the French and English began adding milk to their hot chocolate.

It was not until the 19th century that the cacao bean's real evolution occurred, when the precursors of our modern processing techniques were invented and "eating chocolate" was first produced. Machines for grinding beans were invented and the process no longer had to be done by hand. In 1928 in Holland, Coenraad Van Houten patented his chocolate press, which was far more effective than earlier techniques at separating the fat, or cocoa butter, from the ground beans, leaving behind dry cakes that could be ground into cocoa powder. Hot chocolate made from this powder was much less oily and greasy than what they'd been drinking in Europe until Van Houten's invention; he also developed the process called Dutching: adding an alkali to the acidic cocoa powder. Dutching darkens the color of cocoa powder, mellows and deepens its flavor and makes it dissolve more easily. Van Houten's company paved the way for large-scale manufacturing, and soon chocolate was no longer reserved for the monied upper classes.

Cadbury in England and Suchard in Switzerland are some of the now-familiar chocolate firms established early in the 19th century. In the late 1870s, Henri Nestlé and Daniel Peter created the first milk chocolate. At the same time, another Swiss chocolatier, Rudolph Lindt, perfected the technique known as conching, a process that grinds and kneads chocolate into a much more unctuous, less grainy product than had previously been possible, and the modern candy bar, with its smooth texture and mellow flavor, was born.

Today there are cacao plantations throughout the world, centered in the equatorial zone, for cacao trees need tropical conditions to thrive. The origins of the cacao tree are usually traced back 4,000 years or so to the Amazon River basin in Brazil, and Brazil is a major producer, as are West Africa and Malaysia. Other sources are Mexico, Venezuela (once one of the world's largest producers), Ecuador, Colombia and, on a small scale, Hawaii.

The cacao tree is rather odd-looking, for its pods grow out from its trunk and along its larger branches; in addition, it produces flowers and fruit continuously and simultaneously, so that a single tree will have both white blossoms and pods of all sizes and colors, depending on their state of ripeness. Although trees can grow to 40 feet or more, on plantations they are kept to a height of about 20 feet to make harvesting easier.

There are two main varieties of cacao tree, criollo and forastero. The criollo, native to Venezuela, produces the most fragrant, flavorful beans, but the trees are much less hardy than the sturdy forastero, and only a small percentage of the world's supply of cacao beans comes from the criollo tree. However, criollo beans are in demand by many of the best chocolatiers, and efforts have been made to increase supply, in part by revitalizing and upgrading Venezuelan production. There is also a third variety now being cultivated: trinitario, a hybrid of the forastero and

Chocolate-Dipped Strawberries

criollo. It is hardier than the delicate criollo, and its beans are mellower and more flavorful than those of the forastero.

A mature cacao pod looks something like a ridged football, deep orange or yellow in color. Ripe pods are cut from the trees with machetes or special knives and then usually split open with machetes. Some more discriminating producers, however, let the harvested pods age for several days before removing the beans, as this increases their depth of flavor.

A pod contains 25 to 40 beans, each the size of a large almond, encased in a sticky white pulp. Once removed from the pod, the beans are placed in covered vats, or heaped on banana leaves, and covered with more leaves, and left to ferment, a process that begins almost instantly because of the high sugar content of the pulp. After several days the pulp evaporates and the beans are spread out in the sun to dry. (Some producers use ovens to dry their beans, but sun-drying is vastly preferable.) As they dry, over a period of several days, the beans darken in color to various shades of brown. Once dried, they are packed into burlap bags and shipped to the factory for processing.

At the factory, the beans are first sorted, graded and cleaned, then roasted at temperatures ranging from 250° to about 300° F for 30 minutes to an hour, sometimes longer. The best beans are roasted at lower temperatures for shorter times, as both higher temperatures and longer roasting can turn them bitter; judging the perfect temperature and timing is part of what determines how good the resulting chocolate will be. The roasted beans are then cracked and winnowed, which

In a way, chocolate is like wine — or coffee.
It is difficult to say which [chocolate] is the best.
A connoisseur will be familiar with them all and will know the subtle differences. Everyone does not agree; it is a matter of taste.
Just because they look like chocolate, don't expect them all to be alike, any more than wines or coffees are alike.

— Maida Heatter

blows away the outer husk, leaving the inner kernels, called the nibs. In a process somewhat reminiscent of the cuvée used for Champagne, different batches of beans, up to six or eight in all, are combined in specific blends. Again, arriving at the perfect blend is a determining factor in the quality of the final product, requiring a skill not unrelated to that of a Champagne master. (Perhaps it's not so surprising then that aficionados use some of the same terms as wine connoisseurs to describe the taste of their favorite chocolate, speaking of its fruitiness, its complexity, its subtle "notes." And France's Valrhona has introduced special couverture chocolates that it calls its "Grand Crus.")

Once the beans have been blended, they are milled, during which process they are ground and heated at the same time, to melt the cocoa butter and reduce the nibs to the chocolate liquor, or chocolate paste. This bitter paste is essentially the equivalent of baker's, or unsweetened, chocolate, although it is much grainier at this point than the refined product we know. From here, the chocolate liquor continues on one of two paths.

To make cocoa powder, the chocolate liquor is ground again, then pressed to remove much of the cocoa butter (which is reserved for chocolate making). The dry mass left after the cocoa butter is extracted is called a press cake; it is cooled, then crushed, ground finer and sifted: The result is unsweetened cocoa powder. If the cocoa is to be Dutched, via Van Houten's process, the alkali may be added either before or after the chocolate liquor is pressed and ground.

To make chocolate, the cocoa butter is left in the chocolate liquor and other ingredients—such as additional cocoa butter, sugar and/or milk solids—are mixed into the paste. It is then further refined and finally conched, Lindt's process gives the chocolate its meltingly smooth consistency ("mouth-feel," as it is called) that makes it so good. During conching, the chocolate is heated and slowly kneaded over a period ranging from hours to several days. The longer it is conched, the smoother the chocolate becomes; some of the

best producers conch their chocolate for four days or even longer.

The last step in the process is tempering, which gives chocolate its characteristic sheen. Chocolate is basically an emulsion of cocoa butter in chocolate liquor, and tempering stabilizes this emulsion. The chocolate, still warm from the conching process, is cooled, then reheated to a specific temperature, depending on the type of chocolate (e.g., milk or bittersweet). (The emulsion is a somewhat fragile one, which explains why chocolate you melt for a glaze, for example, and then cool is not as shiny as it was to start with—unless you have tempered it again.) And finally the chocolate is molded into blocks or bars.

The amount of sugar added, as well as other ingredients, determines the basic type of chocolate, though there may be a broad range of tastes and textures within each category. The USDA regulates the minimum amount of chocolate liquor each type must contain, but doesn't require manufacturers to label products with either this figure or the amount of cocoa butter contained. In Europe, manufacturers are more likely to display this information, especially on the labels of special couverture chocolates, and now some of the better chocolatiers in North America are adopting the practice too.

Open boxes from top, displaying bonbons from Jerbeau Chocolate, Richart Design et Chocolat and Maison du Chocolat.

Plain chocolate with no sugar added is called baker's, or unsweetened, chocolate; it is 100 percent chocolate liquor. Bittersweet and semisweet chocolate are both considered dark chocolate, but semisweet has more added sugar; both also contain added cocoa butter, vanilla (or vanillin, the artificial flavoring) and, usually, a minuscule amount of lecithin, a soy-based emulsifier, for smoothness. Bittersweet and semisweet chocolate must be at least 35 percent chocolate liquor. What is called sweet chocolate contains at least 15 percent, and up to 35 percent, chocolate liquor. Milk chocolate, which is sweet chocolate with added milk solids, must be at least 10 percent chocolate liquor. And what about white chocolate? The USDA says this can't legally be called chocolate because it contains no chocolate liquor at all. The best "white chocolates," mostly from Europe, are made of cocoa butter, sugar, milk solids and vanilla. Some bars, however, don't even contain cocoa butter but are based on vegetable fat instead; these are often called confectionery coating or summer coating.

Many of the best chocolates, European and North American, contain much higher percentages of chocolate liquor than indicated here. The amount of cocoa butter also varies from brand to brand and product to product. Couverture chocolate—which can be bittersweet, semisweet, milk, or white—is used by discriminating chocolatiers and pastry chefs. French couverture must contain at least 31 percent cocoa butter, which is much more than most eating chocolates contain. France's Valrhona and Belgium's Callebaut are known for their high-quality couverture chocolates. In the United States, Scharffen Berger Chocolate Makers has begun producing a premium chocolate intended to compete with European brands; it contains 70 percent chocolate liquor. And in Venezuela, an up-and-coming company called El Rey Chocolates is now producing high-quality chocolates that are attracting increasing interest from chocolatiers and other connoisseurs.

While a Hershey Bar with Almonds will always have a place in my heart, tastes change. In the past, American chocolates tended to be overly

sweet, sometimes more sugar than chocolate, but now it's easy to find excellent chocolates from both small chocolate makers and some larger companies as well. Many of these chocolatiers have trained with "chocolate masters" in Europe, and their tastes and creations reflect that. For an annotated listing of some of the best chocolatiers, see page 183.

CHOCOLATE MASCARPONE MOUSSE

This rich mousse takes only about 10 minutes to prepare. Just made, it has a light, airy texture; if left to chill thoroughly, it becomes somewhat denser. Either way, it's delicious.

SERVES 4

6 ounces bittersweet chocolate, finely chopped
1 cup heavy cream
1 cup mascarpone
2 tablespoons Kahlúa or
    1½ teaspoons pure vanilla extract

Melt chocolate in a heatproof bowl or in the top of a double boiler over simmering water, stirring frequently until smooth. Remove from heat and let cool until tepid.

In a large bowl, whisk cream and mascarpone until smooth. With electric mixer, beat until mixture just holds soft peaks; do not overbeat. With rubber spatula, stir in about ¼ cup of mascarpone mixture into chocolate until smooth. Fold in remaining mascarpone. Stir in Kahlúa. Serve immediately, or cover and refrigerate until ready to serve (mousse can be made up to 1 day ahead).

An assortment from L.A. Burdick Chocolates.

Lots of choc'late for me to eat…
— Eliza Doolittle
in My Fair lady

CHOCOLATE-RASPBERRY TART

Raspberries and chocolate are one of my favorite combinations. In this elegant tart, the fresh raspberries sit on a layer of rich chocolate ganache flavored with black raspberry liqueur.

SERVES 8

TART SHELL
1 1/2 cups all-purpose flour
3 tablespoons confectioners sugar
1/8 teaspoon salt
6 tablespoons chilled unsalted butter, cut into 1/2-inch cubes
About 2 1/2 to 3 tablespoons ice water

FILLING
6 ounces bittersweet chocolate, coarsely chopped
1/2 cup plus 2 tablespoons heavy cream
1 tablespoon Chambord liqueur

1 1/2 pints raspberries
1 ounce bittersweet chocolate, melted

In a food processor, combine flour, confectioners sugar and salt, and pulse to blend. Add butter and pulse until mixture resembles coarse meal. Add 2 1/2 tablespoons ice water and process just until dough starts to come together; if necessary, add another teaspoon or so of water. Shape dough into a disk, wrap in plastic and refrigerate for 20 to 30 minutes, or until firm enough to roll.

On a floured work surface, roll out dough to a 12-inch round. Fit dough into a 9-inch fluted tart pan with removable bottom and trim off excess dough. Refrigerate 20 to 30 minutes.

Richart Design et Chocolate's silk-screened chocolates.

Position a rack in lower third of oven and preheat to 400° F. Line tart shell with foil, leaving an overhang, and fill with dried beans, rice or pie weights. Bake 15 minutes. Remove foil and weights and bake 10 to 12 minutes longer, until tart shell is lightly golden brown. Transfer pan to a wire rack and let cool completely.

In a food processor, finely chop chocolate. In a small saucepan, bring cream to a boil. With processor running, add hot cream to chocolate and process about 20 seconds, until completely smooth. Transfer to a bowl and let cool about 5 minutes, then stir in Chambord. Let cool until just beginning to thicken, 10 to 30 minutes (depending on the chocolate).

Scrape filling into cooled tart shell and smooth top. Working from the outside in, arrange raspberries in concentric circles on the ganache. Refrigerate for 1 hour, or until filling is set.

Drizzle melted chocolate over top of tart in a decorative pattern. Serve, or refrigerate until ready to serve (tart can be prepared up to 1 day ahead).

CHOCOLATE SILK PIE

This old-fashioned favorite has a wonderfully rich, satiny-smooth chocolate filling.

SERVES 8

PASTRY

1 ⅓ cups all-purpose flour

3 tablespoons granulated sugar

⅛ teaspoon salt

8 tablespoons (1 stick) chilled unsalted butter, cut into ½-inch cubes

About 2 ½ tablespoons ice water

FILLING

3 ounces bittersweet chocolate, coarsely chopped

1 ounce unsweetened chocolate, coarsely chopped
12 tablespoons (1 ½ sticks) unsalted butter, at room temperature
1 cup superfine sugar
1 ½ teaspoons pure vanilla extract
3 large eggs, at room temperature
Chocolate curls or shavings for garnish

In a food processor combine flour, sugar and salt, and pulse to blend. Add butter and pulse until mixture resembles coarse meal. Add 2 tablespoons ice water and process just until dough starts to come together; if necessary, add another teaspoon or so of water. Shape dough into a disk, wrap in plastic and refrigerate 20 to 30 minutes, or until firm enough to roll.

On a floured work surface, roll out dough to a 13-inch round. Fit dough into a 9-inch pie pan. Trim overhang to ½ inch, fold overhang under itself and crimp to make a decorative edge. Refrigerate 20 to 30 minutes.

Position a rack in lower third of oven and preheat to 375°F.

Line pie shell with foil, leaving an overhang, and fill with dried beans, rice or pie weights. Bake 15 minutes. Remove foil and weights and bake 10 to 12 minutes longer, until pie shell is lightly golden brown. Transfer pan to a wire rack and let mixture cool completely.

In small heatproof bowl or in the top of a double boiler set over barely simmering water, melt chocolate, stirring occasionally until smooth. Let mixture cool slightly.

In large bowl, using electric mixer, beat butter and superfine sugar until light and fluffy, about 3 minutes.

Beat in vanilla, then beat in melted chocolate. Beat in eggs one at a time, beating for 5 minutes after each addition (this is important!).

Scrape filling into cooled pie shell and smooth top. Refrigerate until set, at least 4 hours, or overnight.

Before serving, scatter chocolate curls over top of pie and cut into wedges. (Refrigerate any leftovers.)

CHOCOLATE TRUFFLE CAKE

Serve this rich, dense cake with a garnish of fresh raspberries if you like.

SERVES 6

6 ounces bittersweet chocolate, coarsely
  chopped
3/4 cup sugar
1 teaspoon espresso powder
Pinch of salt
6 tablespoons boiling water
12 tablespoons
(1 1/2 sticks) unsalted butter,
  cut into 12 pieces, at room temperature
3 large eggs, at room temperature
1 1/2 teaspoons pure vanilla extract
Confectioners sugar for dusting
Sweetened whipped cream for serving

Preheat oven to 350º F. Grease a 6 1/2-inch springform pan. Line bottom with a round of parchment or waxed paper and grease the paper.

Combine chocolate, sugar, espresso powder and salt in food processor, and process until finely ground. With machine running, add boiling water and process until chocolate is completely melted, 10 to 15 seconds. Scrape down sides of bowl, add butter and process until mixture is smooth. Add eggs and vanilla and process just until well blended. Scrape batter into prepared pan and smooth top.

Bake 40 to 45 minutes, until edges of cake are puffy and center is just set and no longer wet-looking. Cool cake in pan on a wire rack for 30 minutes (cake will crack and sink as it cools), then cover and refrigerate at least 3 hours, or overnight.

To serve, run a thin-bladed knife around edge of cake, then remove sides of springform. Invert cake onto a serving plate, carefully remove bottom of pan and peel off paper. Dust top of cake generously with confectioners' sugar. Cut into wedges and serve with whipped cream.

ULTIMATE HOT FUDGE SAUCE

This thick, fudgy sauce with undertones of caramel is irresistible—it's meant to be served hot over ice cream, but if you have leftovers, you may find yourself eating it cold straight from the bowl.

MAKES ABOUT 1 1/4 CUPS

1/2 cup heavy cream
4 tablespoons unsalted butter, cut into 4 pieces
1/2 cup packed light brown sugar
Scant 1/4 cup granulated sugar
Pinch of salt
1/2 cup Dutch-processed cocoa
1/2 teaspoon pure vanilla extract

Combine cream, butter, sugars and salt in heavy medium saucepan and bring to a simmer over medium heat, stirring to dissolve sugar. Reduce heat to medium-low and simmer for 2 minutes. Reduce heat to low, add cocoa and whisk until smooth. Transfer to a bowl and stir in vanilla. Serve over ice cream. (Leftovers can be reheated in a double boiler over barely simmering water.)

One of Larry Burdick's signature chocolate mice (and ribbon-tied wooden box).

CHOCOLATE-DIPPED STRAWBERRIES

Of course you can use one chocolate only, if you'd rather, but dark-chocolate-dipped and white-chocolate-dipped berries look prettier side by side on the plate.

MAKES 12 STRAWBERRIES

12 very large strawberries with
  stems (about 1 pound)
2 ounces bittersweet chocolate,
  finely chopped
2 scant teaspoons vegetable
  shortening
2 ounces white chocolate,
  finely chopped

Rinse strawberries, drain on paper towels and pat thoroughly dry. (If possible, clean berries an hour or so before dipping them, drain, pat dry and refrigerate, then pat dry again when ready to proceed—any moisture will make melted chocolate "seize" into an unworkable mass.) Line small baking sheet with waxed paper.

In a small bowl, melt bittersweet chocolate with 1 scant teaspoon of shortening, stirring until smooth. If chocolate seems too runny, let cool briefly. Dip 6 berries 3/4 of the way into the chocolate, turning to coat evenly. Lay berries on baking sheet.

Melt white chocolate with remaining 1 scant teaspoon shortening and dip remaining 6 berries. Place baking sheet of berries in refrigerator just until chocolate is set, about 5 minutes.

Carefully remove berries from waxed paper and arrange on serving plate. Serve, or cover loosely and refrigerate for up to 8 hours.

FOIE GRAS

*My idea of heaven is eating pâtés de foie gras
to the sound of trumpets.*

—Sydney Smith

The French term *foie gras*, literally translated, means "fat liver," and refers to the livers of specially fattened geese and ducks. Although France is the country most closely associated with it, foie gras, like many of the other delicacies in this book, has a very long history. No one knows how it was first discovered that geese and ducks that gorged themselves would develop oversize and delicious livers, but bas-reliefs dating back to at least 2,500 BC depict Egyptians force-feeding geese with balls of packed grain. The Romans liked to indulge their geese with a diet of figs so that the birds' overdeveloped livers would take on the sweetness of the fruit. It was during the Roman occupation of Gaul that its residents first developed their taste for foie gras.

In France, Gascony, Alsace and the Périgord are the regions known for foie gras. *Foie gras d'oie* is goose foie gras, *foie gras de canard* is duck foie (from, respectively, Strasbourg or Toulouse geese and, traditionally, Barbary or Muscovy ducks, and now moulards as well). Each bird has its partisans, although goose foie gras has been the traditional favorite. However, personal preferences aside, most connoisseurs agree that each is

When in France...

In contrast to the large-scale self-contained operation at Hudson Valley Farms in the United States, foie gras production in France remains in many ways a cottage industry. Of course there are commercial producers, but throughout Gascony, Alsace and the Périgord, you will see hand-lettered signs offering foie gras as well as other regional specialties, at many small farms. Some of these farms also offer "foie gras weekends," where you can learn about, goose foie gras, confit de canard and the like, while enjoying a taste of farm life and good country home-cooking. One such farm is that of Danie and Guy DuBois, at La Dornac in the Dordogne. Patricia Wells calls the farm "the best address I know for excellent homemade *foie gras d'oie*," and chocolatier Richard Donnelly of Donnelly Chocolates told me theirs was "the most luscious foie gras" he has ever tasted. (For information, contact Danie and Guy Dubois, Peyrenegre, 24120 Ladornac, Terrasson-la-Villedieu; phone, 53.51.04.24; fax, 53.51.11.22.)

best treated differently in cooking. Goose foie gras is even richer than duck foie gras, and more of it melts away if cooked at high temperatures; therefore it's better for terrines, for example, which are baked at a low temperature. Duck foie gras holds up better to sautéeing and high-temperature roasting.

Throughout southwestern France, once geese and ducks being raised for foie gras reach the age of five months or so, they undergo a four- to five-week period of *gavage*, or forced feeding, before they are slaughtered. (Whether this is inhumane or not seems to depend on who you talk to.) The ducks are fed twice a day, but geese must be fed more often; raising geese can be

problematic in other ways as well. The result of this intensive feeding, usually with corn, is livers several times the size of those in the average bird—up to 2 $\frac{1}{2}$ pounds for a goose, 1 $\frac{1}{2}$ pounds or more for a duck.

Of course, the liver is not the only part of the bird that is used; in the markets of small towns throughout southwestern France, you will see the meaty birds (minus their livers), preparations of *confit d'oie* or *confit de canard* and other delicacies, as well as the livers, for sale. Although foie gras and the fattened ducks and geese may appear in the markets from late October to April, November and December are the prime months, and foie gras is a traditional part of many French Christmases and New Year's celebrations.

Although France has long been the main source of foie gras, it is also produced in Israel, Hungary, Poland, Canada and, since the last decade, the United States. Until the mid-1980s, the only foie gras available in the United States was canned, because the Department of Agriculture prohibits the importation of fresh foie gras into the country—and there certainly wasn't anyone producing it here. In 1982, however, Izzy Yanay, an Israeli who had experience in the foie gras business in his country, and a partner started a foie gras farm in upstate New York. The farm began producing in its very first year; in part, their success stemmed from the fact that they were raising a "super duck," the moulard, a sturdy hybrid of the Muscovy and the Pekin, or Long Island, duck. (The technique for crossbreeding the two had been developed a few years earlier in Israel and, through unrelated efforts, in France.) However, there was no market for the farm's foie gras—even upscale restaurants had been able to serve only the processed canned foie gras or mousses, and most people didn't know how good fresh foie gras could be.

But then Yanay met Ariane Daguin, daughter of André Daguin, a well-known chef in Gascony, foie gras country. She knew all about foie gras, and in 1985 she and partner George Faison started a company called D'Artagnan in Jersey City to market Yanay's foie gras to top New York restaurants and other customers. They also solved the problem of what to do with the rest of the duck: D'Artagnan now produces fresh foie gras terrines and mousses, and also sells magret (the meaty breast from a foie gras duck), confit and a variety of other "by-products." (See Resources, page 185.)

Hudson Valley Foie Gras, Yanay's current operation, in business since 1989, remains one of only two foie gras producers in the United States. Sonoma Valley Foie Gras, in California, is the other. Proprietors Guillermo and Junny Gonzalez began producing foie gras from Muscovy ducks in 1986. The Gonzalezes, who are from El Salvador, learned their skills from Danie and Guy Dubois, at their foie gras farm in Perigord (see Box, page 108). Sonoma is a smaller operation than Hudson Valley, but it offers foie gras terrines and mousses, magrets, duck prosciutto and the like, in addition to fresh foie gras. (See page 185 for mail-order information.)

Ironically, in light of the somewhat bewildered reception American foie gras first received (although its quality has never been in question—even top French chefs working in this country, including Jean Louis Palladin from Gascony, the foie gras heartland, rate it highly), *The New York Times* published a story shortly before Valentine's Day, 1998 about the "foie gras crisis," i.e., shortage. It reported that producers couldn't keep up with the demand from restaurants and other customers across the country, with orders triple or more what they were just a few short years ago.

Buying and Cooking Foie Gras

In the United States, foie gras is graded according to USDA standards. Grade A livers, the best, must weigh at least 1 pound; most are at least $1\frac{1}{4}$ pounds and some are as large as 2 pounds. Grade A livers are pale beige; they are the least veiny and have an exquisite silky smooth texture when cooked. Grade B livers weigh between 8 ounces and 1 pound and are darker than As. Although grade Bs can be good, they have more blemishes or imperfections than grade As and are veinier. Grade Cs are 8 ounces or under, with the

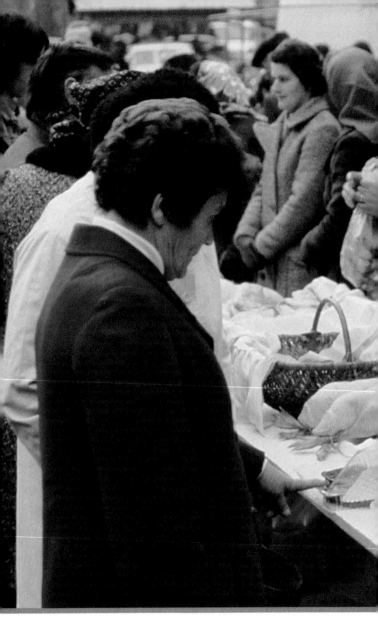

Foie gras market in France.

most blemishes and veins; they are not, in fact, sold to consumers and are likely to be reserved for commercially processed mousses and similar products. The best foie gras is just firm to the touch. It shouldn't be spongy, which means it has a comparatively low fat content and will be difficult to sauté.

The classic way to prepare foie gras is to bake it into a terrine, often after marinating it in Sauternes or a similar wine. However, there are many other ways to serve it, as innovative chefs

in both France and North America have discovered. Sauteed medallions of foie gras, seared on the outside and meltingly smooth inside, are delicious, as is foie gras roasted at a high temperature to the same effect. Because foie gras is so rich, it takes well to sharp, acidic, astringent flavors. Wolfgang Puck's (chef/owner of Spago) foie gras garnished with pineapple is a well-known example. Christian Delouvrier, chef of New York City's Les Célébrités, has served a foie gras "burger"—a sautéed medallion sandwiched between the top and bottom of a halved roasted lady

But It's Good for You

In case you were worried about what feasting on foie gras might do to your cholesterol level, fear not. Several years ago, *The New York Times* reported on the result of a ten-year study that focused on the Gascon diet, finding that it was higher in saturated fat than diets anywhere else in the industrialized world. But at the same time, it turned out, the Gascons have the lowest rate of death from heart disease in France—about a quarter of what it is in the United States. As the scientist in charge of the study pointed out, goose and duck fat is more similar to olive oil than to butter. And then of course there's all that healthful red wine they drink, too.

apple. Above-mentioned chef André Daguin includes a variety of imaginative recipes in his book, *Foie Gras, Magret, and Other Good Food from Gascony*, from sautéed foie gras with radishes to a foie gras cured in salt. He also prepares foie gras with green grapes; his dish of the whole liver steamed over crushed grapes and wine is very contemporary, but, interestingly enough, the combination of tart grapes and rich liver appears in *Larousse Gastronomique*. *Larousse* also includes that other classic presentation, foie gras and truffles. Truffles provide a delicious, earthy counterpoint to the delicate texture of the liver, which is why foie gras mousses and terrines studded with black truffles are so popular.

Preparing Foie Gras

When confronted with a whole foie gras, here is what to do. French recipes call for soaking the liver in ice water for several hours to remove any traces of blood, but that is usually unnecessary with duck livers produced in this country. However, if preparing a terrine or roasting or cooking the foie gras whole, you will want to remove the veins. This is easier to do if the liver is not ice-cold, because it might break apart in the process. (Let it sit at room temperature for about 30 minutes before deveining it, then return it to the refrigerator until ready to cook)

Each liver has two lobes, one larger than the other; carefully separate them, cutting the connective vein if necessary. Peel off any thin membranes remaining on the liver, remove any white fat on the inner part of the lobe, and trim off any greenish spots, which would taste bitter. Each lobe has a larger vein running lenthwise through the center and a network of smaller veins radiating from it. If you're lucky, you can find the end or center of the central vein and pull it out, but it's more prudent to gradually remove it, working along its path with your fingertips; be careful, though, or you'll end up with pieces. (Because of the texture of foie gras, however, you can more or less press it back together if need be.) If you are slicing the foie gras for sautéeing, deveining is more a matter of personal preference; it's often better just to slice it, then remove any noticeable veins with tweezers. For neat slicing, use a hot knife, dipping it into hot water and wiping it clean between slices.

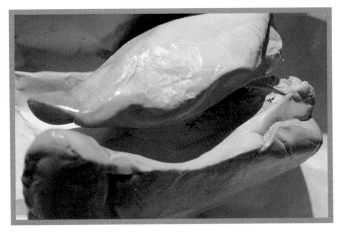

A whole foie gras, separated into two lobes.

Pan-seared foie gras served with Sauternes.

Château d'Yquem
Sauternes

Sauternes & Other Foie Gras Wines

Sauternes, the sweet white wine from Burgundy, has traditionally been considered the classic accompaniment to foie gras, whether used in the preparation of a terrine or chilled, poured and served. The Sauternes from the exalted Château d'Yquem are perhaps the best known, and they deserve to be; these wines are so fine they have their own classification, *premier grand cru* — the only ones to be so designated. But about two dozen other châteaus produce Sauternes premiers crus or seconds crus in a region slightly south of the city of Bordeaux. The district encompasses five communes: Sauternes, Barsac, Bommes, Preignac and Gargues. Sauternes is unusual in that its sweetness is entirely natural, the result of a mold *(botyrtis cinerea)*, known as "noble rot" that attacks the grapes late in the season. The mold causes the grapes to shrivel on the vine, which, through dehydration, concentrates their natural sugars. In addition, the grapes (mainly sémillon and sauvignon blanc, with a small proportion of muscadelle) are allowed to overripen, which means they are left on the vine until very late in the harvest — with the risk of an unexpected frost destroying the crop before it is picked. Harvesting is also arduous; the progress of the mold varies from bunch to bunch, so there are often at least six and as many as 12 individual pickings in one vineyard. And in some years, either the mold doesn't appear or the harvest does not meet the château's standards (in which case the grapes may be picked earlier and used for dry wines, or harvested late but used for "generic" Sauternes, without a château's name on the label). But when conditions are right, the "noble rot" results in some noble wines, smooth, honeyed and delicious.

There is no one best wine to serve with foie gras, because the choice really depends on the way the dish is prepared: A red wine with some acidity can be delicious with sautéed or roasted foie gras, while a gewürztraminer might be just right for a foie gras dish with Asian flavors.

ROASTED FOIE GRAS WITH SHERRY VINEGAR SAUCE

Roasting foie gras at high temperatures sears and browns the exterior while leaving the inside meltingly smooth. The idea for this delicious sweet-sharp sauce came from Anne O'Hare, talented chef/proprietor of New York City's Azure restaurant.

SERVES 8 AS AN APPETIZER

$3/4$ cup sugar
$1/4$ cup water
$3/4$ cup plus 2 tablespoons sherry vinegar
1 fresh duck foie gras ($1\,1/2$ to $1\,3/4$ pounds),
   deveined (see Box page 116)
Salt and freshly ground black pepper
$1/2$ teaspoon coarsely ground black pepper,
   or more to taste

Place a rack in upper third of oven and preheat to 475° F.

Combine sugar and water in medium heavy saucepan and bring to a boil over medium heat, stirring to dissolve sugar. Brush down sides of pan with wet pastry brush to remove any sugar crystals and boil without stirring, until a deep golden caramel color, 5 to 7 minutes. Remove from heat and add sherry vinegar (be careful—the caramel will bubble up). Return pan to medium-low heat and cook, stirring with wooden spoon, until any lumps of caramel dissolve and sauce is completely smooth. Set aside.

Lightly oil a large cast-iron skillet or small roasting pan. Season foie gras with salt and pepper, place in pan and roast for 6 to 7 minutes, until it begins to brown. Carefully turn foie gras and roast for about 6 minutes longer, or until well browned and metal skewer inserted into center comes out just warm to the touch. Transfer foie gras to a plate and cover to keep warm.

Pour off fat from pan and set skillet over medium heat. Add sauce and bring to a simmer, scraping up any browned bits from bottom of pan. Simmer until sauce is slightly reduced and thickened, 2 to 3 minutes. Stir in coarse pepper, season to taste with salt and remove from heat.

Slice foie gras and arrange on serving plates. Drizzle a little sauce over foie gras and serve immediately. Pour remaining sauce in a small sauceboat.

Sautéed Foie Gras with Cranberry Chutney

SERVES 8 AS AN APPETIZER

This spicy chutney, with its citrus tang, is the perfect counterpoint to the richness of foie gras. The recipe makes more chutney than you'll need, but refrigerated it keeps for at least two weeks. Serve with roasted chicken or other poultry; it is particularly good with squab or other game birds.

DRIED CRANBERRY CHUTNEY

1 $^3/_4$ cups dried cranberries (about 7 ounces)
1 large Granny Smith or other tart apple, peeled, cored and finely chopped
1 large onion, minced
1 garlic clove, minced
1 to 2 jalapeño peppers, minced
2 teaspoons grated ginger
$^1/_2$ cup cider vinegar
$^1/_4$ cup orange juice
$^1/_4$ cup water
$^1/_2$ cup packed brown sugar
$^1/_2$ teaspoon salt
1 tablespoon red wine vinegar
Salt and freshly ground black pepper
3 tablespoons olive oil
1 fresh duck foie gras (1 $^1/_2$ to 1 $^3/_4$ pounds), deveined if desired (see Box page 116)
4 ounces mesclun or other mixed greens (about 6 cups)

What the Label Means

In France, the labeling of foie gras products is very strictly regulated by law. Here are some terms you will see on tins or jars of such products:

Foie gras (*d'oie* or *de canard*) *entier* means a whole lobe, with a smaller piece or two added if necessary to reach the necessary weight. If the can says just *foie gras d'oie* or *de canard*, it contains large pieces of a lobe, not a whole one. A *bloc de foie gras* gras is processed puréed pieces of the liver; a *bloc avec morceau* must contain visible pieces of the lobe within the purée. Once the amount of foie gras drops below 100 percent, the product can no longer be labeled foie gras, but must be identifed rather as just *foie d'oie* or *foie de canard*. A *parfait de foie* is puréed foie gras that may contain added fat and puréed chicken livers, but must be a minimum of 75 percent foie gras. *Pâtés*, *galantines* and *purés* or *mousses* contain a minimum 50 percent foie gras, with the remainder made from pork, veal, chicken, and pork and chicken livers.

Even the use of the word for truffle is strictly legislated. If *truffle* appears on the label, it must contain at least 3 percent truffles; less than that and the percentage must be specified, for example, *truffe a 2%*.

Other terms include *foie gras cru*, or raw fresh foie gras—the best, but not what you would want to bring back on the plane. *Foie gras mi-cuit* or *foie gras frais* has been only briefly cooked—not enough to allow you to bring it legally into the United States. *Foie gras semi-conserve* has been cooked and pasteurized, foie gras en conserve has been sterilized as well.

Combine all ingredients for chutney in a large heavy nonreactive saucepan. Stir well and bring to a simmer over medium-high heat, stirring occasionally. Reduce heat and simmer, stirring occasionally, until apple and onion are very soft, 25 to 30 minutes. Remove from heat and let cool. Put in bowl and then refrigerate until ready to serve.

In a small bowl, combine vinegar, $1/2$ teaspoon salt and $1/8$ teaspoon pepper. Gradually whisk in olive oil until well blended. Set aside.

Using a long sharp knife, cut foie gras on the diagonal into 8 slices. Season on both sides with salt and pepper. Heat two large heavy skillets over medium-high heat until hot. Add foie gras and cook until golden brown on bottom, 1 to $1 1/2$ minutes. Turn foie gras and cook until golden brown on second side, about 1 minute longer. Transfer to paper towels to drain and cover loosely with foil to keep warm.

In large bowl, toss mesclun with vinaigrette. Arrange salad on 8 serving plates, placing greens near top of each plate. Place foie gras just below salads, spoon a generous dollop of chutney next to each slice and serve immediately.

[on Christmas dinner]:
To start with?
Well, here I think you can be nontraditional,
and I almost always am.
If I can afford it,
I like to start with fresh foie gras or caviar.
This spells celebration to me....
If I have foie gras,
I either want a very cold, almost frappé bottle
of Sauternes, or a favorite fine Champagne —
and plenty of time
to linger over it....
—James Beard

Pasta with Morels and Foie Gras

*Don't be tempted to use fresh pasta here—you want the contrast
of the firmer texture of dried pasta against silky-smooth foie gras.
Use a good-quality imported semolina pasta such as Barilla.*

SERVES 4 AS AN APPETIZER

1 tablespoon unsalted butter
1 shallot, minced
8 ounces morels (or other wild mushrooms),
  trimmed, thoroughly rinsed and halved or
  quartered, depending on size
Salt and freshly ground black pepper
$2/_3$ cup chicken stock
$3/_4$ cup heavy cream
3 tablespoons finely chopped flat-leaf parsley
10 ounces imported bow tie (farfalle) pasta
8 ounces fresh duck foie gras, cut into $1/_2$-inch cubes
  (see Note)

While bringing a large pot of salted water to a boil,
melt butter in a large deep heavy skillet over medium-
high heat. Add shallot and cook, stirring, until translucent, about 2 minutes. Add morels, season with salt
and pepper and cook, stirring, until mushrooms have
softened and most of their juice has evaporated,
about 5 minutes. Add chicken stock, bring to a gentle
boil and cook until most stock has evaporated, about
5 minutes. Add cream, bring to a simmer, reduce
heat and simmer until sauce is slightly reduced and
thickened, 2 to 3 minutes. Stir in parsley and adjust
seasoning. Remove from heat and set pan aside.

Add pasta to boiling water and cook just until al
dente, about 10 minutes; drain.

About 5 minutes before pasta is cooked, heat a
large cast-iron or other heavy skillet over medium-
high heat until hot. Season foie gras with salt and
pepper, add to pan and cook, stirring frequently until
just beginning to brown, about 1 minute. Remove
pan from heat and, with a slotted spoon, transfer foie
gras to paper towels to drain.

Reheat sauce over medium-low heat. Add pasta and heat, tossing frequently, about 1 minute, to allow it to absorb some sauce. Add foie gras, toss well and serve immediately.

NOTE: Although the idea would be sacrilege to some, it is possible to freeze "extra" foie gras (if there should be such a thing). Wrap it first in plastic wrap, then in foil, and keep in the coldest part of freezer for up to 2 weeks. I've sometimes used the larger lobe for roasting or slicing and sautéeing, then frozen the smaller lobe to use for this pasta.

SMOKED SALMON

Although smoked salmon does not inspire the same kind of exalted reverence as some of the other delicacies in this book, it is certainly one of our favorite indulgences. And it pairs so well with certain of these other delicacies too: Think of a few slices of smoked salmon topped with crème fraîche and caviar, served with a flute of chilled brut Champagne.

There are two basic ways of preparing smoked fish: hot-smoking and cold-smoking. For either method, the fish is first cured in a salty brine or with a dry salt rub. This is a preservative measure but, depending on their composition, brines or rubs may also be used to add flavor to the fish. With a brine, the curing process is shorter, since the brine penetrates the flesh of the fish more quickly than a dry cure; depending on the size and type of fish, it may be cured for only an hour or so, or up to six hours or more. Fish that is dry-salted may be cured for a minimum of eight to ten hours up to a period of two days or more. At Perona Farms in New Jersey, sides of salmon are dry-cured for between three and four days. The proprietor, Kirk Avondoglio, has been quoted as saying "wet-brining is cheating," a point of view that certainly has its proponents,

"Designer" Salmon

Although different smokehouses have always experimented with different brines or rubs to flavor their smoked salmon, recently some of the flavorings have been rather on the exotic side. "Pastrami" salmon is one of the more successful of these experiments. David Burke, chef of New York City's and Chicago's Park Avenue Cafés, was responsible in large part for popularizing pastrami-style salmon, which is cured with the same spices and flavorings used for pastrami, including coriander, paprika, cayenne, black pepper and molasses (Perona Farms, produces Park Avenue Cafe's pastrami salmon). Other flavorings include lemon dill, cilantro and tequila, juniper berry and vodka and pepper. Purists may be horrified, but some of these brines are really quite delicious. (A different kind of "designer" salmon is four-star-chef Daniel Boulud's private-label smoked salmon, produced by Browne Trading Company.) See page 185 for sources.

although not everyone would agree. While many of the long-established European firms, in Scotland and Norway, for example, rely on dry-curing, others use the brining method; most of the excellent smoked salmon produced in North America has been cured with a brine.

With either method, after curing the fish is rinsed and left to air-dry (or fan-dry) for several hours or more, long enough to develop

[on Thanksgiving dinner]:
...and I like something very simple
but very expensive first: caviar, if I can afford it,
otherwise delicious smoked salmon...
— James Beard

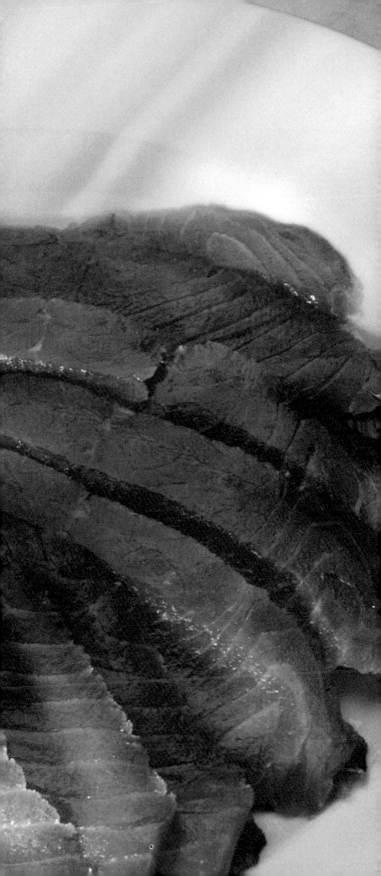

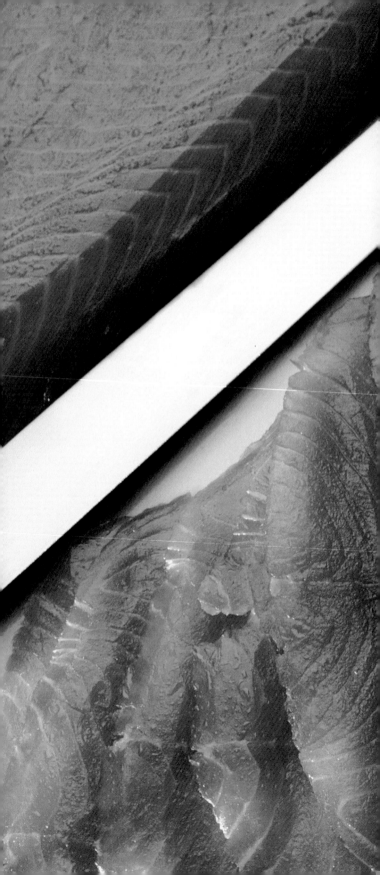

What Is Lox, Anyway?

Although lox, traditional partner to bagels, may frequently be thought of as smoked salmon, usually it's not. The name comes from a German word for salmon, *lachs* or *laks* and actually refers to brined Pacific salmon. These days, the term is often used to mean the smoked (or sometimes only cured, not smoked) salmon called Novy or Nova. While this name refers to Nova Scotia salmon, its original source, it is simply called Nova at the deli counter and is often quite salty.

what is called the pellicle. This very thin, shiny skin helps keep the fish moist during smoking and prevents an unappetizing white "curd" from forming.

Hot-smoking usually takes less time than cold-smoking, which actually dries the fish rather than cooking it. Fish is hot-smoked at temperatures between 125° and 180°F. Generally, the temperature is gradually increased over the smoking period; higher temperatures of course are more likely to dry out the fish. Different producers rely on different combinations of temperature and timing for the results they seek. Cold-smoking is done at temperatures under 90° F, over a period of anywhere from less than 24

*Fishing for salmon on the River Avon
at Tomintoul, Scotland.*

Sides of fresh Scottish salmon. A. H. Jarvis and Sons, Kingston upon Thames, Surrey.

hours up to three days or more. Some producers keep the temperature very low, drying the fish at only 65° to 70° F or so.

Hot-smoked salmon has a different texture from cold-smoked. Although some fish is better hot-smoked, hot-smoked salmon tends to crumble rather than slice nicely into gossamer-thin, delicate sheets, so it must be cut into chunks or per-

haps crumbled into scrambled eggs rather than sliced. Because those gossamer slices of salmon are so desirable, most high-quality smoked salmon is cold-smoked. However, hot-smoked salmon, which is more popular in the Pacific Northwest, can be delicious.

Whether fish is hot-smoked or cold-smoked, the type of fuel is obviously essential to the final result. Hardwoods and fruitwoods are the woods of choice, in chips or as sawdust. Among the favorite

hardwoods are oak, hickory, maple, alder and juniper. The preferred fruitwoods include apple, cherry and pear. Most Scottish salmon is oak-smoked; in *Fish & Shellfish*, author James Peterson points out that the fuel for the best Scottish smoked salmon is recycled oak barrels that have been used for aging whisky. Many producers use a mix of woods to achieve the flavor they want, varying it according to the type of fish. Often the smoker indicates on the package the type of wood or the mix used, which is helpful if you know you like certain flavors more than others.

Gutting and cleaning salmon caught in Loch Fyne, Argyll, Scotland.

A smokehouse can be anything from a jerry-rigged homemade affair to a huge state-of-the-art plant. Inside are racks or shelves for the fish and/or hooks to hang it from, and the heat source for the smoke; for cold smoking, the heat source is separated from the fish and the smoke is piped into the area where the fish is kept. Some commercial smokehouses welcome visitors, so you can view the process for yourself. And if you

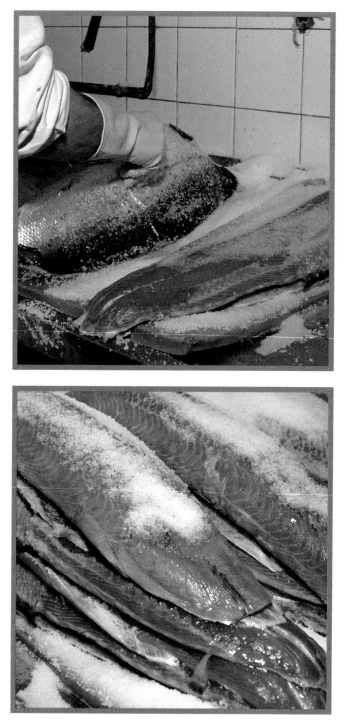

Salting sides of Scottish salmon in order to draw out the moisture before smoking.

Salmon is first cured in salt and brown sugar and then smoked in small kilns over old whisky cask chips. Loch Fyne, Argyll, Scotland.

want to try your hand at smoking your own fish, James Peterson's *Fish & Shellfish* provides good instructions on how to do it (so does A. J. McClane's *Encyclopedia of Fish Cookery*, but it's out of print now and not easy to find).

The "best" smoked salmon is a matter of personal taste, but whether it is imported or produced in North America, certain characteristics are desirable. The fish should have good color and look neither dried out nor overly oily. It should taste moist, almost buttery, with a silky-smooth texture. Some people like a strong smoky flavor, others prefer a milder taste of smoke, but in any case, the smoked flavor shouldn't overpower the salmon. Nor should the fish taste overly salty, although this is in part a matter of taste; most Irish and Scottish smoked salmon is saltier than that from North America.

The variety of salmon used also affects taste, at least to a certain extent. But although smoked wild salmon, particularly wild Scottish salmon,

Sides of Scottish salmon being smoked while hanging from hooks in the traditional way. A. H. Jarvis and Sons, Kingston upon Thames, Surrey.

was once unquestionably the best, this is not necessarily true today—(fortunately, considering the realities of the supply of wild salmon). Today, both North American and European smoke-houses are producing very high quality smoked salmon from farmed fish. Incidentally, the terms "Scottish-smoked," "Irish-smoked," etc., on imported smoked salmon mean that the fish used was Atlantic salmon; northern European producers import a lot of Pacific salmon for smoking as well, but in that case, the fish will just be called "smoked" rather than identified as Scottish, Irish and so forth. (For sources for smoked salmon, see page 185.)

Smoked Sturgeon and Friends

There are a few other smoked fish that can keep company with smoked salmon; the fish that produces caviar is one. Smoked sturgeon, which can be either hot- or cold-smoked, has a mild, delicate flavor and a meatier texture than smoked salmon. Look for both imported smoked sturgeon from the Caspian Sea and California and Oregon's smoked white sturgeon, farmed or wild. Smoked tuna can also be excellent, and, of course, there's smoked trout, the best of which can be very fine. (See page 185 for sources.)

Hand slicing of sides of smoked salmon at A. H. Jarvis and Sons, Kingston upon Thames, Surrey.

Smoked Salmon & Accompaniments

Minced red or white onions
Capers
Chopped hard-boiled eggs—yolks and whites
  chopped separately
Crème fraîche or sour cream
Lemon wedges
Dill sprigs or chopped chives

Variations: If you are serving a "designer" smoked salmon, you may want to vary the garnishes accordingly. For example, for cilantro-tequila smoked salmon, substitute small sprigs of cilantro for the dill and very finely minced jalapeño chiles for the capers (or flavor the crème fraîche with a few drops of the juice from a jar of hot peppers). For juniper berry-smoked salmon, lace the crème fraîche with a bit of gin. For pastrami smoked salmon, serve thinly sliced rye bread instead of brioche.

Mini Smoked Salmon-Corn Fritters

These addictive little fritters are good on their own, but the crème fraîche and chives dress them up a bit. If you really want to indulge, garnish with top-quality salmon caviar.

Makes about 4 dozen hors d'oeuvres

$1/2$ cup all-purpose flour
$5/8$ teaspoon baking powder
$3/4$ teaspoon salt
$1/8$ teaspoon freshly ground black pepper

6 tablespoons milk
1 medium or large egg
1 tablespoon unsalted butter, melted
1 3/4 cups fresh corn kernels (about 3 ears)
3 ounces smoked salmon, thinly sliced, finely diced
2 tablespoons diced red bell pepper
1 tablespoon finely chopped chives,
  plus extra for garnish
Vegetable oil for frying
About 2/3 cup crème fraîche

In a medium bowl, stir flour, baking powder, salt and pepper together. In another medium bowl, combine milk, egg and melted butter. Add to dry ingredients and stir until well blended. Stir in corn, smoked salmon, bell pepper and chives until well mixed.

In large heavy frying pan, heat 1/4 inch of oil over medium-high heat until oil is very hot but not smoking. Drop batter by generous teaspoonfuls into hot oil, without crowding. Flatten each fritter slightly with spoon back and cook until golden brown on bottom, 1 to 2 minutes. Using a slotted spoon or spatula, turn fritters and cook until golden brown on both sides, about 2 minutes longer. Transfer to paper towels to drain, and repeat process with remaining batter. (These are best served as soon as they are made but if necessary can be kept warm on a paper towel-lined baking sheet in a 200° F oven for up to 30 minutes. To make things go more quickly, cook fritters in two frying pans.)

Top each fritter with a generous 1/2 teaspoon crème fraîche, garnish with chopped chives and serve immediately.

Potato Galettes with Smoked Salmon & Caviar "Gâteaux"

This recipe was inspired by a smoked salmon, crème fraîche and caviar appetizer we served at Manhattan's Sign of the Dove restaurant when I worked as a cook there. In this version, the crisp potato galettes are a nice contrast to the silky salmon and smooth cream. The caviar mixture can be made several hours in advance and refrigerated.

<small>SERVES 4 AS AN APPETIZER</small>

1 medium baking potato (about 10 ounces; choose an evenly shaped potato)
1 1/2 tablespoons unsalted butter, melted
Salt and freshly ground black pepper
Generous 1/2 cup crème fraîche
1 tablespoon chopped chives, plus extra for garnish
1 1/2 tablespoons salmon caviar
4 large slices smoked salmon (about 6 ounces)

Preheat oven to 400° F.

Peel potato. Using a mandoline or sharp knife, cut potato into 1/8-inch-thick slices. You will need 36 slices; discard smaller end pieces.

Generously grease large heavy baking sheet with some of the melted butter. Toss potato slices with remaining butter. Arrange slices on baking sheet to make 4 galettes: For each, start with one slice in the center, then arrange 8 overlapping slices in a circle radiating out from the center slice like the petals of a flower. Sprinkle with salt and pepper and bake about 15 minutes, or until edges begin to brown and potatoes are cooked through; turn pan once or twice for even browning.

Meanwhile, in medium bowl, combine crème fraîche and chives. Gently stir in salmon caviar and season to taste with salt and pepper. Cover and refrigerate.

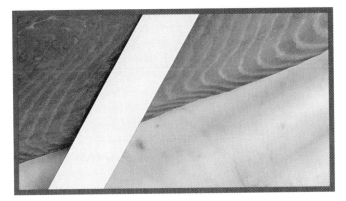

Smoked
Salmon
&
Accompaniments

Smoked salmon with its classic
accompaniments makes a simple but elegant first course.
Two or three slices (about $1\frac{1}{2}$
ounces) per person is a reasonable amount; you can simply
offer small bowls of the different accompaniments, allowing
your guests to serve themselves
as they prefer, or you can garnish each plate individually. If
you like, serve a sliced brioche
loaf or thinly sliced good white
bread.

Smoked Salmon "Tartare"

You can prepare all the ingredients several hours in advance. Refrigerate them separately, covered, until ready to serve, but don't prepare the tartare until just before serving, or the acidic lemon juice will start to "cook" the smoked salmon, affecting its taste and texture. Garnish each serving with sevruga or salmon caviar if you like.

SERVES 4 AS AN APPETIZER

$3/4$ pound smoked salmon, thinly
   sliced, cut into $1/4$-inch dice
$1/4$ cup minced red onion
2 tablespoons small capers
2 tablespoons chopped chives
1 tablespoon fresh lemon juice,
   or to taste
Freshly ground black pepper
Chopped chives, plus 8 to 12
   chive "sticks" ($1 1/2$- to 2- inch
   lengths), for garnish
Chopped dill for garnish

In a medium bowl, combine salmon, onion, capers and chives and mix well. Add lemon juice and pepper to taste. Gently pack $1/4$ of the mixture into a lightly oiled small rounded cup or very small bowl, then unmold onto center of serving plate. Repeat with remaining salmon mixture. Stick a few chive sticks into the center of each mound of tartare and sprinkle chopped chives and dill around each serving.

153

Wild salmon by a stream in Scotland.

To serve, using a spatula, carefully transfer galettes to serving plates (rearrange slices if necessary). Mound crème fraîche mixture in center of galettes, and wrap a slice of salmon around each mound. Garnish with chopped chives and serve immediately.

SMOKED SALMON DIP

Serve with crackers (black-pepper water crackers would be a good choice) or mini toasts —or, if you're feeling ambitious, gaufrette potatoes or homemade potato chips.

MAKES ABOUT 2 CUPS

2 cups crème fraîche
4 ounces smoked salmon, thinly sliced, minced
3 tablespoons chopped chives, plus extra for garnish
2 teaspoons vodka
Salt and freshly ground white pepper

In a medium bowl, combine crème fraîche, salmon and chives. Stir in vodka and season to taste with salt and white pepper. Cover and refrigerate for 1 to 2 hours to allow dip to firm up slightly.

To serve, transfer to serving bowl and sprinkle chopped chives over top.

TRUFFLES

The truffle is not an outright aphrodisiac,
but it may in certain circumstances
make women more affectionate
and men more amiable.
—Alexandre Dumas

Brillat-Savarin called truffles black diamonds, Colette referred to them as jewels, French epicure André Simon asserted that "truffles, of course, are not a vegetable; they are a miracle." What is it about truffles that makes people rhapsodize so? Fresh from the earth, a black truffle doesn't look particularly imposing, and fresh white truffles are if anything even more unprepossessing in appearance. (In his *Harry's Bar Cookbook*, Arrigo Cipriani tells the story of a woman he saw pick up an "exotic crudité" from a bowl near the bar to munch on with her drink: "I asked her if she liked it. 'Not really,' she said. I replied, 'You've just eaten one hundred dollars' worth of truffles.'")

But truffles have a long history as a gastronomic delight, and there is nothing to compare with their intense, musty, intoxicating fragrance, the aroma that makes truffle fanciers practically swoon with delight. The truffle has been credited with aphrodisiac powers, and feasting on truffles (even if the feast is less than an ounce of truffle) can be a sensual experience. Wine writer Matt Kramer says the reason for their mysterious, almost mythical appeal is simple: "Truffles are the perfume of the earth itself." Alexander Dumas once wrote that, if asked what it was, a truffle would respond, "Eat me and adore God."

The Romans were well acquainted with truffles, and Apicius's cookbook, from the first century AD, contained several recipes for truffles. Well-known British food writer Elizabeth David refers to the "ironic picture" in Pliny's *Natural History* of "Roman gentleman preparing mushrooms with

their own hands—the only cooking they ever condescended to do."

Although there are numerous varieties of truffles, it is the black truffle from France's Périgord region, *Tuber melansoporum*, and the white truffle, *Tuber magnatum*, from Italy's Piemonte, that are by far the most highly prized. The black truffle is traditionally associated with Périgord, primarily the Dordogne and Lot districts, but today

Historically, sows were used to hunt for truffles.

much of the harvest comes from Provence. The town of Alba, in the Langhe district of Italy's Piedmont region, is the center of the white truffle business, but despite the reputation of the Piedmontese truffle, many of the white truffles on the market today come from Umbria and other regions farther south. Each has its own champions, but white truffles are generally considered both more fragrant and more delicate.

The way truffles grow and are harvested explains much of their mystique. For one thing, intensive scientific explorations notwithstanding, the reasons why truffles thrive in one particular spot, reappearing year after year, and not in another, are still not completely understood. Although truffles are often thought of as a fungus, like mushrooms, they are actually the fruit of the fungus, or *mycorrhizae*. They grow underground (and, unlike mushrooms, they never emerge from the earth), close to the roots of trees such as oaks, poplars, willows and some nut trees, among others, that flourish in chalky soil. The fungi have a symbiotic relationship with these trees that somehow allows them both to thrive; most attempts at cultivating truffles have been based on recreating this relationship. Then, because truffles remain hidden underground, they must be detected by their scent—hence truffle hounds and, historically, truffle-hunting pigs. The image of a huge sow unearthing the treasure of a truffle is a captivating one, but pigs enjoy truffles too, and they want to eat their finds; these days they have been replaced by dogs, who aren't really interested in eating truffles but can be trained to detect them.

The seasons for both white and black truffles is short: December to March for the black, October to late January for the white. The climate affects the growing cycle: If the previous spring has been dry, preventing development of the precious spores, the outlook for the harvest is not good. A wet and relatively cool early fall is desirable, and if there's little rainfall then, the harvest will be disappointing. (Generally, a good year for wine is a bad one for truffles, and vice versa.) For other reasons as well, in both France and Italy, harvests are much smaller than they were even 20 or 30 years ago. Truffle forests have been cut down, truffles have been overharvested or carelessly harvested and pollution has taken a toll too.

The truffle hunter's task has never been an easy one, and now demand and competition for finding truffles is even more intense. (In recent sea-

Sows have been replaced by dogs in the hunt for truffles.

sons in Italy, there have been reports of truffle dogs being poisoned). Secrecy has always been a hallmark of truffle hunting—and often of disposing of the precious haul as well. Truffles tend to reappear in the same spot year after year, and the truffle hunters, not surprisingly, want to keep the spots they know about to themselves. So the *tartufai*, or in Piemontese dialect, *trifolau*, in Italy and *les éleuéurs de truffes*, or *caueurs*, in France do their work alone at night, under cover of darkness. With their dogs, they revisit places that have been fruitful before, and if they are lucky, the dog sniffs out a truffle that must then be carefully unearthed. If the dog has located a truffle that is too small, the soil can be gently replaced to allow it to grow—often amazingly quickly—to a more desirable size.

If you're in Italy or France in the right season, you may encounter one of the many truffle fairs held in small and large towns. Alba, not surprisingly, has one of the larger fairs, during the first week or two of October. As Carol Field writes in *Celebrating Italy*, "You know you've come at the right time

when your nostrils are assaulted by a wild, intoxicating aroma that perfumes the air." Almost every restaurant serves truffles, and the truffle markets are in full swing. Later in the year, there are similar festivities in the Dordogne and throughout the Périgord region, where there are major truffle markets in Sarlat and in Périgueux, among other towns. Keep in mind, however, that much of the real buying and selling goes on behind the scenes or at unlikely hours in both France and Italy, and some of the more serious markets are not open to tourists or the general public.

Cultivation of Truffles

Although large-scale commercial cultivation of truffles remains a highly unlikely scenario, there has been some success in this area. There are two main approaches, the first a time-honored one known in France since early in the 19th century. Basically it involves planting oak trees in an area known to be receptive to truffles and waiting for the trees to grow, with the expectation that truffles will be found among their roots. Jacques Pébeyre, acknowledged as the leading *trufficulteur* in France—he's often been called "the king of

truffles"—has relied on this method, among others, for years, as have other farmers throughout France's truffle regions, and the same method has been attempted in various parts of the United States as well. But recently there have been advances in the search for a more reliable method; the other approach that seems to have validity involves using "truffled trees." These are young seedlings of specific trees known to be friendly to truffles, usually oaks, that have been inoculated with truffle spores before planting. In

If I can't have too many truffles,
I'll do without truffles.

—Colette

Farmer sorting truffles.

recent years, Italy's Urbani Tartufi, the world's largest supplier of truffles, has raised thousands of these truffled seedlings in greenhouses; the seedlings have been planted all over Italy and in France. Similar experiments are being undertaken in the United States as well, in Texas and a few other states.

Tuber Aestivum and Other Relatives

Besides the French *truffe noir* or *truffe du Périgord* and the white Italian *tartufo bianco*, or

Delicate negotiations at the truffle market.

tartufo d'Alba, there are several other kinds of truffles. *Tuber melanosporum*, the same species as the French black truffle, does grow in Italy, but for some reason, they do not taste the same. Found in both Piedmont and Umbria—and sometimes called Norcia truffles, after the Umbrian town where the best come from—they are less flavorful and less fragrant than France's black truffles. (Most Italian cookbooks, in fact, barely mention black truffles—in Italy, "tartufo" really means the white truffle.)

"Summer truffles" (*Tuber aestivum*), occasionally called English truffles, look like black truffles but are really only a pale imitation of the real thing. They don't have as much flavor, and most truffle lovers would rather get their out-of-season truffle fixes with truffle oil or similar products rather than settling for summer truffles. Some markets try to pass off summer truffles as *Tuber melansporum*, although any reputable shop, of course, will differentiate, sometimes even labeling true black truffles "winter truffles."

In the United States, you may also come across the Oregon white truffle, *Tuber gibbosum*. These are smaller than Italian white truffles but can be aromatic and flavorful. (A member of the North American Truffling Society told me that James Beard, who was born in Portland, was quite fond of Oregon white truffles.) The Oregon black truffle is actually a member of another genus, *Leucangium carthusianum* (until very recently, this was classified as *Pico carthusiana*, (which most

references call it). Larger than European black truffles, it has a less intense flavor, and has not, as of yet been marketed commercially.

… There is nothing much better
in the Western world
than a fine, unctuous, truffled pâté.
—M. F .K. Fisher

Buying and Cooking Truffles

Whether you are buying a white or a black truffle, it should be firm to the touch and its fragrance immediately apparent. Sponginess indicates age, and if a truffle isn't aromatic, you don't want it. Although you can keep truffles for a few days at home, it's best to use them as soon as possible. You can simply put them in a tightly sealed container in the coldest part of the refrigerator, but there are better ways to keep a truffle, which offer some added benefits. In gourmet shops you may see truffles displayed in baskets or containers of rice. The rice helps keep truffles fresh, so there is logic as well as aesthetics behind the presentation. At home, though, you can store the truffle in rice the same way—covered and in the refrigerator—and after even just a day, you will have rice infused with truffle aroma.

The same trick works with eggs, another food with which truffles share an affinity. Put a truffle in a jar with a few eggs still in their shells and store in the refrigerator; you will have truffled eggs, which you can cook on their own, or with some of the truffle (save the rest to use with another "non-truffled" ingredient). You can also store black truffles in Cognac or other brandy or liquor, which will become infused with truffle scent.

You could, in fact, infuse a liquor the same way with a white truffle, but since white truffles are best used fresh and raw, it doesn't seem the wisest use of them. While black truffles are more often cooked, although paper-thin slices of raw black truffle may be shaved over a dish for garnish or added to a salad, white truffles may be

Aromatic truffles sautéeing.

*Presently we were aware of an odour
gradually coming towards us,
something musky, fiery,
savoury, mysterious —a hot, drowsy smell,
that lulls the senses and yet enflames them
—the truffles were coming...*
—William Thackeray

warmed but are almost never cooked. The heat of a dish of risotto, for example, will bring out the overpowering aroma of white truffles shaved over it, but with too much heat, the fragile fragance will disappear.

Scrambled eggs with black truffles is a classic combination and a favorite French dish; in Italy, fresh tagliatelle showered with shaved white truffles, and the aforementioned risotto, are classics. (In fact, there are special sharp-bladed slicers designed just for slicing truffles paper-thin; they are available in specialty cookware shops.) White truffles and rich cheese can be a heady combination; a regional specialty of Piedmont is *fonduta*, a creamy sauce/"fondue" of Fontina cheese, milk and eggs, often finished with a shaving of white truffles. *Poularde en demi-deule* is another traditional French dish made with black truffles, in which truffle slices are stuffed under the skin of a plump chicken and allowed to infuse their flavor before cooking. A dish prepared *à la périgourdine* will often feature both truffles and diced foie gras. Jean-Louis Palladin's *Cooking with the Seasons* includes an eight-course truffle tasting menu that finishes with, yes, black truffle ice cream, which he acknowledges was inspired by André Daguin, the Gascon chef known for his artistry with foie gras. And if you think truffle ice cream is intriguing, you may be interested in the "truffled truffles" a French chocolate shop has created. With "truffle king" Jacques Pébeyre, chocolatier Henri Le Roux created a chocolate truffle studded with fresh black truffles, which has won awards in France.

Canned Truffles and Other Products

Although high-quality canned black truffles can certainly be good, they will never be as good as a fresh-from-the-ground truffle. However, since the latter is often not an option, if you do buy canned or jarred truffles, splurge and get the best: large whole truffles rather than pieces or shavings. Actually, I think frozen truffles (commercially frozen, that is) are far superior to canned. Both white and black flash-frozen truffles are available via mail order from Urbani Truffles (see Resources). Among other truffle products available through mail order and in specialty gourmet shops are truffle oils, both black and white. High-quality oils are a good source of that elusive fragrance: White truffle oil is delicious drizzled over prosciutto, for example, and will take humble mashed potatoes to new heights, while black truffle oil is a lovely garnish for a plate of carpaccio. And good-quality truffle butters can be wonderfully fragrant, stirred into hot fresh pasta, tossed with gnocchi or used to finish a sauce. (See page 185 for sources for truffle products.)

Recipes

MUSHROOM RISOTTO WITH WHITE TRUFFLES

This risotto is one of the favorite ways to celebrate truffle season in Italy.

SERVES 4 TO 6 AS AN APPETIZER

2 tablespoons olive oil
6 ounces small cremini mushrooms, trimmed and
  thinly sliced
Salt and freshly ground black pepper
5 to 6 cups chicken stock (or two 14 $^1/_2$-ounce cans
  low-sodium chicken broth plus enough water to
  make 6 cups)
1 onion, minced
1 $^1/_2$ cups Arborio or other risotto rice
$^1/_2$ cup dry white wine
4 tablespoons unsalted butter, cut into 4 pieces,
at room temperature
$^2/_3$ cup freshly grated Parmesan cheese
1 $^1/_2$ to 3 ounces white truffles

Heat 1 tablespoon of oil in a large deep frying pan over medium-high heat. Add mushrooms, season with salt and pepper and cook, stirring frequently until mushrooms are tender and liquid has evaporated, 6 to 8 minutes. Scrape mushrooms into a bowl and set aside.

Meanwhile, in a large saucepan, bring stock just to a simmer. Reduce heat and keep at a bare simmer.

Wipe out skillet, add remaining 1 tablespoon oil and

Away with all this slicing, this dicing,
this grating, this peeling of truffles!...
eat it on its own, scented and grainy-skinned,
eat it like the vegetable it is,
hot and served in munificent quantities.

—Colette

heat over medium heat. Add onion and cook, stirring until translucent, about 3 minutes. Add rice and cook, stirring to coat with oil, until rice begins to turn opaque, about 2 minutes. Add wine and cook, stirring until the liquid has been absorbed by rice. Add about $1/2$ cup of hot stock and cook, stirring, until the stock has been completely absorbed by rice. Liquid in frying pan should bubble gently as you stir; adjust heat as necessary. Continue to cook, adding stock $1/2$ cup at a time as the previous addition is absorbed and stirring constantly until rice is tender but still firm and risotto is creamy, 20 to 25 minutes longer. With last addition of stock, stir in mushrooms. (If using broth/water mixture, you may not need it all.)

Remove from heat and stir in butter and Parmesan. Season to taste with salt and pepper. Spoon risotto onto serving plates and shave truffles over the top. Serve immediately.

TRUFFLED SCRAMBLED EGGS

These creamy French-style scrambled eggs are not quite as rich as Scrambled Eggs with Caviar (page 000) —the better to let the truffle's essence shine through. If you haven't "truffled" your eggs by storing them with a truffle, whisk the eggs together with the minced truffle and let sit for about 30 minutes before cooking to infuse them with flavor.

SERVES 2

5 large eggs
$1/2$ to 1 ounce black truffle, thinly sliced or minced
1 tablespoon heavy cream
Salt and freshly ground black pepper
1 tablespoon unsalted butter

In medium bowl, beat eggs, truffle, cream and salt and pepper to taste. Melt butter in medium frying pan over low heat. Add eggs and cook, whisking constantly, until eggs are very creamy and just set, about 5 minutes. Spoon onto two serving plates and serve immediately.

TAGLIATELLE WITH WHITE TRUFFLES

The first time I ever had white truffles was when a friend and I were served this dish at Da Ivo Restaurant in Venice. The chef himself grated the truffles —a lot of truffles —over the hot pasta, and we were hooked. For a slightly less rich dish, you can simply toss the tagliatelle with melted butter and grated cheese before topping with truffles.

SERVES 4 TO 6 AS AN APPETIZER

³/₄ pound fresh tagliatelle or fettuccine
²/₃ cup heavy cream
3 tablespoons unsalted butter
6 tablespoons freshly grated Parmesan cheese
Salt and freshly ground pepper
1 ¹/₂ to 2 ounces white truffles

Bring a large pot of salted water to a boil. Add tagliatelle and cook just until al dente, 2 to 3 minutes; drain.

Meanwhile, in a large skillet, bring cream and butter to a simmer. Simmer until cream is very slightly reduced, about 1 minute.

Add pasta to cream, toss to coat and heat over low heat, stirring occasionally, for about 1 minute, to allow pasta to absorb some sauce. Add cheese, season to taste with salt and pepper and toss again. Transfer to four plates, shave truffles over the top, and serve immediately.

RESOURCES

Chocolates

Chocolaterie Bernard Callebaut
1313 1st Street S.E.
Calgary, Alberta
Canada T2G 5L1
(tel) 800-661-8367;
      403-265-5777
(fax) 403-265-7738

Bernard Callebaut, the fourth generation of the famed Belgian chocolate family, more than does justice to his heritage. Some of his more unusual creations include a white chocolate truffle flavored with maple syrup liqueur (The Canadienne) and two disks of dark chocolate sandwiching an Avocaat-flavored buttercream filling (The Bernard). The less-erotic choices, such as the espresso-dark chocolate truffle, are equally delectable, and the caramel and toffee fillings are wonderful. Callebaut (who now has shops in the United States as well as Canada) also offers holiday specialties, chocolate drops for chocolate chip cookies), dessert sauces (including caramel), and, not surprisingly, bars of couverture chocolate.

Chocolats Le Français
269 South Milwaukee Avenue
Wheeling, IL 60090
(tel) 847-541-1317
(fax) 847-541-7489

At the restaurant Le Français, known as one of the best in America, chocolatier Jim Graham creates exquisite chocolates, predominantly ganache-filled, with such flavorings as lemongrass, Earl Gray tea and mint. The whipped caramel filling is delicious too, and Graham also makes what he calls "fleurons," sort of an upscale version of the familiar chocolate turtle, with roasted cashews, caramel and bittersweet ganache. Other specialties include a rich "hot chocolate creme" and chocolate-covered macadamia-nut toffee.

De Granvelle, Ltd.
347 Madison Avenue
New York, NY 10017
(tel) 800-9-BELGIUM;
    212-953-8888
(fax) 212-953-7095

This Belgian firm makes chocolates with a number of wonderfully indulgent and unusual fillings, from a buttercream and soft caramel combination to "Irish coffee," with mocha buttercream, fudge and Irish whiskey, in a white chocolate tower. Pâtés de fruits are a specialty, as are marzipan-filled chocolates. The truffles are fabulous, particularly the Grand Marnier and the mocha, and the prices are very reasonable.

Donnelly Chocolates
1509 Mission Street
Santa Cruz, CA 95060
(tel) 408-458-4214
(fax) 408-425-0678

Richard Donnelly is a dedicated artisan chocolatier who makes wonderful, sophisticated chocolates. The Germain Robin brandy ganache, soft caramel, and espresso ganache are some of the more classic fillings, but the unusual coconut ganache and peanut butter ganache are just as delicious; some of the flavors vary from season to season. Individual (just under two ounces) bars of chocolate—such as pure chocolate, orange, and bittersweet and semisweet chocolate mix—are another specialty, and Donnelly's dark chocolate-covered ginger is the best I've ever tasted. The packaging is equally impressive, featuring beautiful and original handmade papers in a variety of designs and colors.

Fran's Chocolates, Ltd.
1300 East Pike Street
Seattle, WA 98122
(tel) 800-422-3726;
    206-322-0233
(fax) 206-322-0452

There is nothing like Fran's Gold Bar, which could be described as the best candy bar in the world: rich smooth caramel studded with toasted whole almonds or macadamia nuts and covered in high-quality bittersweet chocolate. But Fran (Bigelow) also makes truffles (most of which are flavored with liqueurs), creams and other individual chocolates and confections, as well as fabulously indulgent dessert sauces, including caramel and dark chocolate. A recent addition to her selection are premium chocolate bars made with Veneuzuela's El Rey chocolate; they come in several different flavors, and one includes ground cacao nibs for crunch.

Jerbeau Chocolate

1080 Avenida Acaso
Camarillo, CA 93012
(tel) 800-755-3723
(fax) 805-484-2477

Jerbeau produces an amazing variety of chocolates and chocolate specialties of all sorts, with both classic European flavorings and traditional American favorites. There are sleek-looking triangular-shaped chocolates with, for example, Grand Marnier ganache or burnt almond paste centers, and there are pecan turtles, old-fashioned caramels, even chocolate-covered Oreos. They also offer many seasonal and holiday specialties, from hand-painted fudge-filled Easter eggs to shiny red Valentine's Day hearts filled with foil-wrapped chocolate hearts.

Joseph Schmidt Confections

3489 16th Street
San Francisco, CA 94114
(tel) 800-861-8682;
        415-861-8682
(fax) 415-861-3923

Schmidt's hand-decorated egg-shaped truffles are available in many gourmet shops, but he also makes exquisite individual chocolates (in the shape of a cluster of grapes, for example), as well as many holiday specialties and other creations (Schmidt is really a chocolate "sculptor" at heart). The truffles, "slicks," which are decorative filled chocolate disks, and chocolates—in flavors including crystallized ginger, "double latte" and peanut butter praline, as well as more classic ones—are rich and incredibly delicious. The packaging is original, and some of it—ribbon-festooned hand-painted boxes and edible chocolate containers—is stunning. (All the truffles, slicks and a variety of holiday and seasonal specialties are available through mail order; the other chocolates can be purchased at the shop and some select outlets.)

L. A. Burdick Chocolate

P.O. Box 593
Main Street
Walpole, NH 03608
(tel) 800-229-2419;
 603-756-3701
(fax) 603-756-4326

Larry Burdick makes exquisitely crafted chocolates with subtle, sophisticated flavorings: mocha with fennel seed, for example, or clove, as well as more traditional combinations. Although Burdick is a serious artisan chocolatier, among his specialties are his signature whimsical chocolate mice, in white, dark and milk, with colored satin tails. The individual chocolates are quite small, so that a one-pound assortment contains 70 to 75 pieces. And while the assorted chocolates, including mice, are available in regular boxes, they also come in lovely small hinged wooden boxes tied with ribbons and stamped with gold sealing wax.

La Maison du Chocolat

1018 Madison Avenue
New York, NY 10021
(tel) 800-988-LMDC;
 212-744-7117
(fax) 212-744-7141

To many, Robert Linxe's name means perfection, and Jim Graham (see Chocolats Le Français) is just one of the many chocolatiers who have traveled to Paris to study and work with him at La Maison du Chocolat. It was Linxe, in fact, who helped Valrhona develop their line of Grand Cru chocolates. His individual chocolates are elegant indeed; my favorite of all is the Rigoletto, with a filling of caramelized butter. There are many ganache fillings, flavored with orange or lemon, peach or mirabelle plum or scented with herbs, among others. The truffles, either pure chocolate or with Cognac, are delicious. Maison du Chocolat also makes caramels, marrons glacés and other confections.

Leonidas

485 Madison Avenue
New York, NY 10022
(tel) 800-900-CHOC;
 212-980-2608
(fax) 212-980-2609

I can still remember the first Leonidas chocolates I

tasted more than 20 years ago in Brussels, and so I was delighted when the 90-year-old Belgian firm opened a shop in New York. Leonidas offers a wide variety of chocolates with crème fraîche, praline, buttercream, marzipan, caramel and truffle fillings, at exceptionally reasonable prices. The Manon Blanc, coffee-flavored crème fraîche in white chocolate, is the one I like best, and others seem to agree, since the Manon Café (the same cream, with a whole hazelnut) is Leonidas's best-selling chocolate.

Richart Design et Chocolate
7 East 55th Street
New York, NY 10022
(tel) 800-RICHART
    212-371-9369
(fax) 212-371-8930

Richart's fine chocolates really are works of art, as the designs on the top of them are silk-screened. This French firm takes chocolate very seriously, as "Le Petit Livre Blanc de Chocolat" ("the little white book of chocolate") that accompanies some of their collections demonstrates, and they offer more than 80 often unusual flavors, including both "Classics" and "Spices and Herbs": ganache with wild strawberries, praline of hazelnuts with thyme and ganache with green tea and mint, among others. Richart treats its chocolates like precious gems (the shops look like jewelry stores and the "architectural" packaging is impressive), and the prices reflect it.

Caviar, Foie Gras, Truffles, and Smoked Salmon

Browne Trading Company
Merrill's Wharf
260 Commercial Street
Portland, ME 04108
(tel) 207-766-2402
(fax) 207-766-2404

Rod Mitchell Browne is a well-known name in the business and his firm produces chef Daniel Boulud's smoked Scottish salmon as well as, in collaboration with Atlanta chef Guenter Seeger, dry-cured smoked Atlantic salmon. They offer other smoked fish too, including smoked wild sturgeon and tuna bacon. And Browne has a large line of caviars, from "private-stock" beluga (and three other belugas) to golden and royal osetra to American hackleback.

Caviar Russe

538 Madison Avenue
New York, NY 10022
(tel) 800-NY-CAVIAR;
    212-980-5908
(fax) 212-980-5928

Caviar Russe numbers golden sterlet caviar (when available) and Siberian Kaluga caviar among its delicacies, along with the other Caspian Sea caviars, including golden osetra. It also sells Scottish smoked salmon, as well as a caviar butter.

Caviarteria

502 Park Avenue
New York, NY 10022
(tel) 800-4-CAVIAR;
    212-759-7410
(fax) 212-750-0358

158 South Beverly Drive
Beverly Hills, CA 90212
(tel) 310-285-9773;
    in CA, 800-287-9773

Forum Shops at Caesars

3500 Las Vegas Boulevard South
Las Vegas, NY 89109
(tel) 702-792-8560

Caviarteria sells excellent caviar at comparatively reasonable prices. It also offers, when available, several specialty caviars, including golden imperial, an ultra beluga and broken-grain beluga and two "select" osetra caviars. Rather than straight pressed caviar, Caviarteria sells what it calls kamchatka, or demi-pressed caviar, a blend of broken-grain beluga and pressed caviar. It also carries Carolina trout roe, Scottish smoked salmon, smoked sturgeon and other delicacies.

D'Artagnan

280 Wilson Avenue
Newark, NJ 07105
(tel) 800-DARTAGN
    973-344-0565
(fax) 973-465-1870

D'Artagnan is the major distributor in the Northeast for Hudson Valley Farm's foie gras (see next page), and they sell a number of products made from their fresh foie gras as well, including terrines (with and without Sauternes), mousses and "French kisses," prunes marinated in Armagnac and stuffed with foie gras mousse. They also offer fresh and smoked magrets, duck breast pastrami and prosciutto, confit, duck fat for cooking (the catalogue says, "Better than butter!") and a wide range of other culinary indulgences.

Ducktrap River Fish Farm, Inc.
RR #2 Box 378
Lincolnville, ME 04849
(tel) 800-828-3825;
          207-763-4141
(fax) 207-763-4235

Ducktrap offers a wide variety of smoked seafood, including, both cold-smoked and hot-smoked (they call it "smoke-roasted) salmon, smoked tuna and white sturgeon, rainbow trout and mussels and scallops.

Hudson Valley Foie Gras
RR #1 Box 69
Ferndale, NY 12734
(tel) 914-292-2500
(fax) 914-292-3009

D'Artagnan is the major distributor in the Northeast of Hudson Valley's fresh moulard duck foie gras, but for retail sources, you can contact the company itself.

Marché aux Delices
120 Imlay Street
Brooklyn, NY 111231
(tel) 888-547-5471
(fax) 718-858-5288

Marché aux Delices carries a wide variety of delicacies and gourmet treats, including, in addition to a long list of wild mushrooms, both fresh and dried, white and black truffles, truffle juice and white and black truffle butter.

Oven Head Salmon Smokers
P. O. Box 455
St. George, New Brunswick
Canada E0G 2Y0
(tel) 506-755-2507
(fax) 506-755-8883

This small family business produces smoked salmon with an incredibly delicate texture and subtle smoky flavor, and their prices are very reasonable.

Perona Farms Food Specialties

350 Andover-Sparta Road
Andover, NJ 07821
(tel) 800-750-6190;
       973-729-7878
(fax) 973-729-4424

Perona Farms, which grew out of a family restaurant/catering firm, makes wonderful smoked salmon and a variety of other products, including Pastrami Salmon for the Park Avenue Café and Salmon Bacon. The salmon is dry-cured rather than brined and then smoked at very low temperatures.

Petrossian, Inc.

(mail order center)
419 West 13th Street
New York, NY 10014
(tel) 800-828-9241
(fax) 212-337-0007

This well-known French firm sells high-quality caviar with an international reputation (and high prices to match). In addition to its beluga, osetra and sevruga, Petrossian offers such accoutrements as gold "palettes" and silver-handled bone spoons for serving caviar. It also sells smoked salmon from Norway, salmon roe from Russia and a variety of other indulgences.

Sonoma Foie Gras

P.O. Box 2007
Sonoma, CA 95476
(tel) 707-938-1229;
       800-427-4559
(fax) 707-938-0496

Junny and Guillermo Gonzalez produce fresh Muscovy duck foie gras on their farm; along with fresh foie gras, they offer terrines and pâtés made from it. They also sell fresh and smoked magrets, duck confit and other delicacies.

Tsar Nicoulai Caviar

144 King Street
San Francisco, CA 94107
(tel) 800-95-CAVIAR;
    415-543-3007
(fax) 415-543-5172

Importers Mats and Dafne Engstrom (who are the ones who taught the Chinese how to improve the quality of their sturgeon caviar) are now producing high-quality American sturgeon caviar from their farm-raised white sturgeon. In addition to impeccably fresh imported beluga, osetra, and sevruga caviars, they also offer an amazing and delicious giant beluga caviar (at a very reasonable price). And their smoked sturgeon is excellent.

Urbani Truffles USA

29-24 40th Avenue
Long Island City, NY 11101
(tel) 800-281-2330;
    718-392-5050
(fax) 718-392-1704

5851 West Washington Boulevard
Culver City, CA 90232
(tel) 213-933-8202
(fax) 213-933-4235

Urbani, "the" name in truffles, offers a wide range of high-quality selections at quite reasonable prices, from fresh white and black truffles in season to flash-frozen truffles to canned and jarred truffles, along with delicious truffle oils, butters, juices, purées and more (even truffle flour). The truffle-studded Italian semisoft cheese is fabulous, as is a white truffle "fonduta." Urbani also sells other delicacies at good prices, among them caviar, including Kaluga and good American paddlefish and hackleback roe, and Norwegian and Scottish smoked salmon.

Reading List

Apple, R. W., Jr. "Innard Beauty." *Saveur* (Nov/Dec 1995): 106-114.

Beard, James. *James Beard's Simple Foods.* New York: Macmillan, 1993.

Bloom, Carole. "All About Chocolate." *Fine Cooking* (Feb/Mar 1995): 41-45.

Brooks, Karen. *Oregon's Cuisine of the Rain: from lush farm foods to regional recipes.* Reading, MA: Addison-Wesley, 1993.

Coady, Chantal. *The Chocolate Companion: a connoisseur's guide to the world's finest chocolates.* New York: Simon & Schuster, 1995.

Coe, Sophie D. & Michael D. Coe. *The True History of Chocolate.* New York: Thames & Hudson, 1996.

Czarnecki, Jack. *A Cook's Book of Mushrooms.* New York: Artisan, 1995.

Daguin, André & Anne de Ravel. *Foie Gras, Magret, and Other Good Food from Gascony.* New York: Random House, 1988.

Del Conte, Anna. *The Italian Pantry.* New York: HarperCollins, 1990.

Evans, Frank & Karen Evans, eds. *The Cookbook of North American Truffles.* Corvallis: North American Truffling Society, 1987.

Fabricant, Florence. "Chefs Staggered by Foie Gras Crisis of '98." *New York Times,* 11 February 1998, F1.

Field, Carol. *Celebrating Italy.* New York: Morrow, 1990.

Fisher, M. F. K. with Bold Knife & Fork. New York: G. P. Putnam's Sons, 1968.

Friedland, Susan. *Caviar.* New York: Scribner's, 1986.

Goldstein, Darra. "Caviar Dreams." *Saveur* (Jan/Feb 1998): 86-94.

Grigson, Jane. *The Mushroom Feast*. New York: Penguin, 1978.

Grossman, Harold J. *Grossman's Guide to Wines, Beers, & Spirits*. 7th rev. ed. New York: Macmillan, 1983.

Heatter, Maida. *Maida Heatter's Book of Great Chocolate Desserts*. New York: Knopf, 1980.

Herbst, Ron & Sharon Tyler Herbst. *Wine Lover's Companion*. Hauppage, NY: Barron's, 1995.

Herbst, Sharon Tyler. *Never Eat More than You Can Lift*. New York: Broadway Books, 1997.

Jenkins, Nancy Harmon. "White Truffle Fever Makes the Season Glow." *New York Times*, 24 December 1997.

Jolly, Martine. *Le Chocolate*. New York: Pantheon, 1985.

Kramer, Matt. *A Passion for Piedmont*. New York: Morrow, 1997.

Lichine, Alexis. *Alexis Lichine's New Encyclopedia of Wines & Spirits*. 4th ed. New York: Knopf, 1985.

Makay, Ian, comp. & ed. *Food for Thought*. Freedom, CA: Crossing Press, 1995.

McClane, A. J. *The Encyclopedia of Fish Cookery*. New York: Holt, Rinehart & Winston, 1977.

Nish, Wayne. "Understanding Foie Gras." *Fine Cooking* (Dec 1994/Jan 1995): 37-41.

O'Neill, Molly. "Can Foie Gras Aid the Heart? A French Scientist Says Yes." *New York Times*, 17 November 1991.

Peterson, James. *Fish & Shellfish*. New York: Morrow, 1996.

Rapoport, Adam. "The American Foie Gras Gamble Pays Off." *Beard House* (Winter 1996): 33-39.

Rosin, Elisabeth. *Blue Corn and Chocolate*. New York: Knopf, 1992.

Schneider, Elizabeth. "Where the Chocolate Tree Blooms." *Saveur* (Sept/Oct 1995): 96-106.

Schneider, Sally. "Truffles in Black and White." *Saveur* (Nov/Dec 1994): 85-96.

Simon, Joanna. *Discovering Wine*. New York: Fireside, 1995.

Strang, Jeanne. *Goose Fat and Garlic: Country Recipes from South-West France*. London: Kyle Cathie, 1991.

Wolfert, Paula. *The Cooking of South-West France*. New York: Dial Press, 1983.

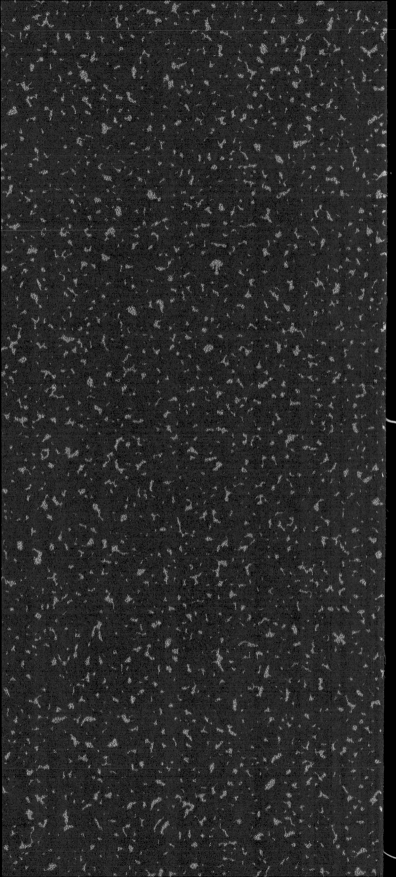